MW00961145

101 DISTRACTIONS FROM DEPRESSION, SELF-HARM
(AND OTHER SOUL-DESTROYERS)

SOPHIA GILL

DISCLAIMER & COPYRIGHT

The information contained in *101 Distractions* is meant to serve as a comprehensive collection of tested strategies that the author of this book has applied to help overcome depression. Summaries, strategies, tips and tricks are only recommendations by the author based on personal experience, and reading this book does not guarantee that one's results will exactly mirror those of the author. All reasonable effort has been made to provide current and accurate information for the readers of this book and the author will not be held liable for any unintentional errors or omissions that may be found.

All rights reserved. No part of this book may be reproduced or transmitted in any form or by any means, electronic or mechanical, including photocopying, recording or by any information storage and retrieval system, without written permission from the author, except for the inclusion of brief quotations in a review.

Copyright © 2013 Sophia Gill
Cover design Copyright © 2013 by Steve Inglis
SANE logo Copyright © 2013 by SANE, www.sane.org.uk

All rights reserved.

ISBN: 1481958232
ISBN-13: 978-1481958233

ABOUT THE AUTHOR

Sophia Gill battled depression for over ten years, during which time she self-harmed extensively. She slowly learned that it was the smaller things in life – simple distractions, which helped her to fight the illness and begin looking at life more positively. Essentially, these distractions gave Sophia an understanding of why and how the illness took hold of her, and gave her the tools to fight it. She is often asked to speak about her experience with mental illness for magazine, newspaper, television and radio, and hopes that her openness will help others to better understand and cope with their own difficulties.

Sophia lives in Church Crookham with her husband, young baby and two cats. *101 Distractions* is her first published book.

CONTENTS

ACKNOWLEDGEMENTS

I wish to personally thank the following people for their contributions and help in creating this book: My husband Mike for his faith, confidence and support, and for patiently listening to my reappearing bouts of paranoia. My father for always believing in my writing and reminding me of my purpose. My mother and sister for simply being there no matter what, and for never judging me when I lost track. I would also like to thank SANE for all of their support and encouragement when it came to speaking openly about depression and writing this book. My child psychiatrist Dr Zwi for getting me through some of my worst years, and never having doubts that I could beat the illness. My GP Dr Jackson for always giving me his time, despite the waiting room queues. My friend Rue for being loyal and solid even when my repetition became tiresome. Finally, I would like to thank every person who emailed, phoned and came up to me in the street to let me know that my interviews about depression and self-harm had helped them in some way. You are the reason I kept writing this book, and are the ones I hope will benefit from its publication. Please don't ever give up hope.

Sophia Gill

FOREWORD

By Marjorie Wallace CBE,
Chief Executive of SANE

I first met Sophia Gill on the set of *This Morning*. We were being interviewed for a piece on self-harm. I was struck by Sophia's attractive personality, warmth and candour. We have remained friends ever since.

Twenty-five years ago when I first started campaigning to improve the rights of people affected by mental health problems, my concern was that the Community Care policy meant, in real terms, that there was too little community and too little care. Has anything changed since that time? Yes. A community of people like Sophia emerged: A community of people affected by mental illness who have come together as artists, writers, and campaigners. Through their chosen medium they offer support and hope, showing that it is possible to journey from a place of extreme mental torment to a better place.

Unlike so many self help books where the premise is that you trade in your old self for a new self, in *101 Distractions*, Sophia suggests you stay with who you are and how you are feeling but seek a practical solution that will help transport you to a different 'headspace'. For example, by reaching out and connecting to other people, interests or activities she shows you can move away from a familiar but unhelpful habit of mind to a more positive outlook.

Sophia's practical suggestions and advice on what helped her through her depression and self-harm is done with empathy and humour. She speaks in the language of the heart: a universal language we can all relate to regardless of why we have mental anguish.

The e-version of *101 Distractions* makes it accessible on your computer or on the go with your kindle, portable phone, or iPad. The format is private and while stigma surrounding mental health still rife, it's understandable that you might not want fellow passengers on the bus knowing what you are reading! The *quick tips*, which Sophia suggests you refer to at the point of need, can be quickly accessed through the media of choice so it makes for a perfect match.

The need for a book like *101 Distractions* has never been greater. Last year alone, there was a four–fold increase in the number of referrals for talking therapies and depression is still a major cause of suicide; sufferers are four times more likely to commit suicide than the general population. SANE campaigns on a macro level influencing government policy and health directives regarding the treatment and care of people with depression while the voices of people like Sophia are needed in equal measure to support the estimated one in five of us who will experience the paralysis of depression at some point in our lives.

INTRODUCTION

Have you ever felt so depressed that you can barely muster the energy to drag your tired body out of bed, never mind find the strength to spend a full day at the office? Do you find yourself crying for no reason, or is someone close to you desperate for your help? Perhaps you understand how addictive it can be to draw a sharp blade across your body, bleeding so that you can try to feel alive.

Depression ate away at my life for over ten years, and at its worst, I coped by cutting my arms several times a day. One of the biggest steps towards my recovery was learning to recognise the signs that I was slipping into that downwards spiral, and distract myself as soon as possible. This allowed me a chance to see that life wasn't just the great grey fog that I had been getting used to, and meant that I could look back and know that there were times when I was OK. If a distraction meant that I didn't self-harm even just for one day, it was a step in the right direction.

At some point in our lives, we will all crave some chicken soup for the soul, top tips for weight loss, or help with that long list of things we should do before we die, but most of the time the useful thing that we really need is a simple, modest distraction.

This is not the book to teach you how to be more assertive, give you recipes to drop a dress size or offer exercises to challenge and train your brain. Nor is it a pair of rose-tinted glasses. This is the book to gently coax you out of the difficult time you are going through, help you find breathing space, and inspire you to find subtle pleasures in life. It is these small things that will help you focus and learn to look at life through a more positive lens.

1

What is a soul-destroyer?

OK so this might not be an official term; more something I created to carefully define everything by one category, but it describes all of those destructive emotions, which literally feel like they are eating away at your soul.

Depression and self-harm were my two main enemies, and they nibbled on my sense of sanity until I felt like I was being rendered useless from the inside out. Without my soul; my sense of personality and self-worth, I was in danger of losing my perspective on life, and for me that would have meant suicide.

You don't have to be someone who self-harms to appreciate this book. You don't even have to be ill with depression. We all have times when life feels pointless and miserable. Your soul-destroyers might stem from the destruction of a relationship or friendship, or perhaps you have lost something or someone. It might be an illness or your work that is the negative element in your life, or there could simply be no reason for the negativity you have found yourself with.

Whatever the outcome of these problems is or could be, they are likely to be equally as crippling as depression was for me, and you mustn't let yourself feel any less justified for needing help.

Changing bad habits to break the downward spiral is incredibly difficult to do, and as always; admitting you even need to change is the brave first step. Whilst the distractions in this book are all fairly obvious ideas, the point of them is in their timing. If you can stop yourself from dwelling on those bad thoughts that are plaguing you, and do any of the 101 distractions in this book instead; even if only for a moment, then you are most certainly heading in the right direction.

How to use this book

This isn't your conventional reading material, and nor is it just a book of lists - although you can use it that way if you need to. It is about seeing how someone else has put each distraction into practice, so that it is easier to understand why each method works. I have tried and tested every single one of the ideas in this book - naturally some more than others, and haven't included anything that I cannot personally recommend.

The snippets of my life in these pages might be just what you need to help you truly believe that you aren't alone, or it might be the insight you are after in order to understand how to help someone else. Whatever it is you need, this book wants to help.

I believe that there are often times when an idea might sound pointless in principle, but as you explore it further the benefits fade into view. Each of these chapters is your fast-track ticket to help you understand why simple actions can help you cope: giving you an easy way to pick out which ideas might work for you.

Distractions can be good for all of us, yet sometimes it can be almost impossible to think of even one thing to do on those days when we feel simply awful.

Now help is here!

You might decide to follow the conventional reading method; start at the beginning and finish at the end. If so, by the last page you should be full of good ideas about how to fight away those negative feelings. Perhaps some of them you had thought of already, but had forgotten about. Or maybe it hadn't occurred to you that some of these distractions might be just what you need. Only you can decide what is right for you.

The book is divided into two sections: short-term distractions and long-term ones. This is to help make your recovery easier, because you can decide whether you need a fast idea to help with the here and now, or if you feel ready to put some more long-term goals in place for the future. As a general rule of thumb, the distractions that can be done no matter what time of day it is are included in the first half of this book. Those that require a little more planning, or are dependent on certain opening hours or some time to practice, come later.

But it doesn't stop there. When you recognise the signs that your personal soul-destroyer is creeping up on you, grab this book and flick to any page. The 'quick tips' are great if you need an idea in a hurry, and offer alternatives for each idea so that you can find something to suit the moment. Whatever distraction you find yourself on, do it. Why not make a promise to yourself to try each distraction at least once? If you don't allow yourself to make excuses, then at very least this book should help you try something new; and that can be extremely refreshing.

To make things easier on the purse strings, each distraction has been given a cost rating. This is displayed as either 'Free' (assuming you already have the relevant items at home which you can use) or with the following piggy banks: -

= Under £5

= Under £50

= 'It's only money'

Naturally some of these could also be done in ways which cost more money, but that part is up to you - there is always something bigger, better and more expensive out there. Simply use these ratings as a starting point. Whilst most of us are on a budget and will be drawn to the cheaper distractions, don't overlook the higher-rated ones. Some of them could be great to plan for in the future, and others you might know how to do for cheaper than I've labelled them.

Remember you don't have to spend money to help yourself. You should be able to work many of the ideas in this book into your day without spending a penny. It's these simple things that we often miss, and yet they can make all the difference.

Hopefully now you can arm yourself to fight away that feeling where you don't see a reason to get out of bed. The reasons do exist. There are 101 of them to be exact.

SHORT-TERM DISTRACTIONS

I used to find that in my worst years, making any form of plan seemed futile. All I craved was an easy way to escape, and for me, suicide felt like my only option. It feels melodramatic to be describing myself with this sort of honesty now, but I know that some will find comfort from the knowledge that someone does understand.

The ideas in this section are designed to be fast and easy to do, without any form of planning or practice involved. They are ideal for those times when you recognise yourself starting to feel trapped by your negative emotions, and are perfect for helping you with the immediate future. They don't require a certain place to be open, and you should be able to try them immediately; no matter what time of day it is.

I know exactly how difficult it is to do anything at all when you feel like this invisible vacuum; a collection of everything that is wrong in the world. I once described this feeling as 'a fire burning in the pit of your stomach. It's filling you with black smoke. Destroying you from the inside. You are afraid to open your mouth, as you know the cloud of misery will engulf those around you. You can't scream because you choke on the darkness. Nothing seems to stop it burning, and you grow weak.'

This weakness will most likely make you feel as though you have no strength to even do the simplest of things - such as get out of bed or dress yourself. However, your recovery has to start with the smallest of steps. I firmly believe that the first one is to distract yourself with something simple, easy, and accessible. You *do* have the strength, and no matter how much your

5

mind tells you that these small feats are impossible or pointless, believe that the opposite is true.

The first chapter in this section is specifically for those who self-harm, and is a collection of the most common distractions used to try and satisfy the urge to damage yourself. Keep using them, even if they only stave off self-harm for a while. A while is better than not at all.

Following this, the next sixty-two distractions are ideas to help you start on that seemingly mythical path to the better, stronger you. Use them at times when you cannot find energy to plan something more long-term. This time will come later on, and the second half of the book is here to help you when that feeling does make its way to you.

SELF-HARM QUICK TIPS

I know all too well how hard it is to control the addiction of self-harm and fight it so that you no longer need to hurt yourself in order to cope. It is an extremely difficult thing to explain and understand, and whilst the distractions in this book are designed to help people who don't necessarily self-harm, I also wanted to include some that are purely based around this issue.

If you are not quite at the stage where you can bring yourself to try the distractions in this book (have faith that you will get there) then please try some of these other ideas to start with. They are quick, specific alternatives to cutting, burning, biting, punching, or any of the other ways in which you currently hurt yourself: -

- Instead of cutting, get a pen and draw on yourself instead. Buy something specifically for this purpose (I find a red pen seems most natural!) and treat it just as you would your usual self-harm tools. Instead of grabbing the knife, scalpel or other blade - grab this pen. It doesn't matter how aggressive you are with it; it will still cause less injury than any kind of blade.

- When you find yourself feeling the aggression that normally leads you towards self-harm, try and let it out by punching cushions, soft toys or teddy bears (sorry Paddington!) Keep doing it until you are exhausted, and don't let yourself be put-off by the fact it sounds silly or obvious.

- Grab some ice cubes out of the freezer and squeeze them as hard as you can. Perhaps hold them against the part of your body where you would normally cut. See if you can break or melt them. You will feel a different kind of pain or discomfort from doing it, but it is an excellent alternative.

- To vent your anger, don't be afraid to scream, shout, holler and wail like a banshee. Who cares if people hear you? Remember that you are the important person here; not that grumpy neighbour who never talks to you anyway.

- Put elastic bands around your wrists, and ping on them instead of self-harming. They will snap against your skin and probably hurt, but this alternative is still one step closer to your goal.

Above all, self-harm is not an intention to kill yourself, and this is the very reason that you must please remember to stay safe. There would be nothing worse than finding you have unintentionally caused more damage than you intended. Learn basic first aid and always treat any wounds. For many people this is all part of the self-harm process, but if you are somebody who simply pulls your jumper over the wound and carries on as normal, your best first step would be to start caring for those injuries. Whilst you might have never had an infection yet, it could be just a matter of time. Also make sure that your tetanus vaccination is up to date.

If you have managed to control the urges by doing one of these self-harm specific things, follow it through by then doing one of the distractions in this book. They are all more long-term ideas that can be used once you start to recognise the signs that you are slipping into that negative pattern. If you keep fighting this, there will be a time when you will turn straight to one of the distractions and you won't even remember the last time you cut. Eventually, you will begin to enjoy doing these things on a daily basis, whether you 'need' them or not.

Remember that this addiction takes a long time to break, so try not to be too hard on yourself. Focus on the time you have managed to not self-harm; even if it just a matter of hours. Unfortunately there is no simple quick fix; but there is a book full of distractions to help.

FREE

1 : PUT ON YOUR RUNNING SHOES

I have a love-hate relationship with running. When I think about it or am asked if I fancy a run, I cringe. Yet when I somehow find myself out there; jogging through the park clutching a bottle of semi-warm tap water in one hand and my large bunch of house keys in the other, slowly I begin to realise that running is actually making me feel better.

It's an age-old saying that exercise is good for us, and try as I might, I simply cannot disprove this well-deserved fact. Yes, my bum would wobble, my thighs would sting, my arms would flail and my knees would beg for forgiveness; but my mind would feel released. It is as if running (and exercise in general for that matter) helps the pain and torment that is in the depressed mind be channelled, churned and expelled through our physical being. Running puts us not only one step closer to the bus stop, but nearer to our recovery from that personal soul-destroyer.

Doing anything that forces your heart to pump a little faster is a natural benefit because it helps your body to produce adrenaline. With your heart beating so strong that you can close your eyes and literally hear that rhythmic pulse, your body responds by feeling alive. Not only an excellent tool against depression, this is an impossible feeling to ignore. In my experience, no matter how hard my negative thoughts would try to sneak past me, every time I've been running I've returned home feeling healthy, positive and empowered.

Quick Tip

- Whether you choose to run around the block, up and down your garden, down the high street or through the park; get yourself out there. Don't forget that well fitted running shoes will make the difference between enjoyment and injury, so do invest in some proper shoes if you intend to give this distraction a real chance.

- If you really can't face running in the outside world; whether it be to locality, weather, or even because you are embarrassed about your current fitness level, there is always the treadmill option. Perhaps it is time to make use of that gym membership? Maybe your partner or friend will also agree to run with you? I always find more enthusiasm for exercise when someone else is there to give me that gentle push.

Remember that it doesn't matter how long you are able to run for. I often only manage a couple of minutes of running, interspaced with a couple of minutes walking. Alternate between the two, and slowly increase the length of time that you run. It's better to do this that to not go out at all.

I would always suggest that you go running even if you don't think that you feel like it. A negative mind will pretty much always make you feel as though you don't want to do anything at all, but if you can get past this initial setback; you will find out that it's quite an insignificant hurdle. After all, this is exactly why distractions are here in the first place: to quash those negative thoughts and get you doing stuff.

FREE TO

2 : WORK THOSE TASTE BUDS

Mmmmm. Just thinking about how best to write this distraction is making me hungry!

The thing is, I truly love good food. My mother taught me many things in life, but the one thing I hold dear to me is that you should never skimp on healthy, wholesome meals. So it might mean paying a bit more for fresh ingredients, but eating right is truly one of the most important things we can do for ourselves.

There are obvious physical health benefits from eating good food, which I'm sure I don't need to explain here, but what we often forget is that this links directly to our state of mind. Put simply, it is much easier to fight mental illness and stay positive, when we are physically strong enough for the fight.

Society has taught us to be very lazy when it comes to food. Lack of time, funds, skill or patience has got each of us grabbing breaded products from the freezer, or dialing the local pizza place to deliver us a fast meal. Even when we try to eat properly, ready-meals lie in wait; tempting us to spend our time doing other things.

Cooking is one of those things which most of us will deny being able to do, but when it really comes to the crunch we would probably all be able to rustle up something to eat. It might not be the best-presented or most healthy meal, but it is a good start.

As a distraction, cooking works brilliantly because when you sit down to eat your concoction afterwards, usually it will fill you with surprise and satisfaction. Being able to make our own meals helps us to try new things and experiment with ideas, and can also help us look at ourselves in a more positive light. I always feel better about what I see in the mirror when I know I've been eating healthily. Plus, we all know that home-cooked food tastes so much better than the bought stuff. So what are we waiting for? Now is the perfect time to start enjoying food.

Quick Tip

- If cooking is totally new to you, ask someone else for help. Your partner, parents, or friends will probably have recipes that they can share, or they might be happy to teach you how to cook a dish or two. Often we relish the chance to feel as though we are passing on some useful tips, so this could be an excellent excuse for some bonding time.

- Cookbooks are another option for beginners and chefs alike, and often they will inspire us to try recipes we'd never considered; or variations of our favourite foods. If you struggle to follow instructions from a book, see if someone has made a video to help, or maybe it's time to watch some cookery shows. I looked for a demonstration video on how to finish the top of a crème brulee with a cooking blowtorch, as I didn't feel as though reading the instructions was good enough. They turned out to be the best puddings I'd ever made!

- Don't forget that this distraction is about the actual act of cooking itself, and so it doesn't matter what you make. Healthy dinners might be good for you, but sometimes getting your knuckles into a greasy cake mix can be much more fun. I went through a real phase of trying to cook various flavours of cupcakes. Sometimes I would come home from work totally depressed, and find myself baking beetroot muffins. How can food so yummy and colourful not bring a smile to your face?

- If preparing your own meals is never going to be something that you choose to do, perhaps instead you can start being more adventurous with the food you buy or the restaurants that you go to. My fiancé, Mike and I used to always be drawn to the same place on our high street, but with a newfound love of Thailand we decided to start trying Thai restaurants. We discovered an amazing restaurant very close to home, and couldn't believe that we'd not been there sooner.

Sophia Gill

FREE

3 : STROKE THE CAT

When I allow myself to quietly remember what depression felt like to me, there is always one strong memory that comes through. I am collapsed on my bed as a great heap. My eyes are stinging and fighting to focus through a great barrage of tears. The fresh cuts on my arms throb and sting; reminders that this time, as always, I was unable to resist. I am alone in the darkness - almost.

My elderly cat; Merlin, and her nearly elderly son; Lancelot, innocently nudge my bedroom door open and spring up onto my bed. Little clumps of cat hair drift down to the carpet behind them; floating on stuffy air. I leap up off my bed to shut the door behind them; afraid that someone might discover this scene and force me to talk. Merlin looks up at me with her big doughy eyes, and softly says 'I love you.' Lancelot rubs the side of his face against my arm, oblivious to any blood transference. He forces my hand out of the way so that he can nest in my lap; showing me that he is along for the ride. They come to me almost as if they are aware of the way I am feeling, and know that I need to be comforted. My tears become a little stronger, as I realise just how lovely my two cats are.

In a strangely calming way, Merlin and Lancelot were my constant link between depression and 'the real world,' and their presence reminded me that I did, and was loved. They helped me to appreciate the good things I had - even if this was simply about loving their purrs and cuddles. On days when I felt unable to face anything at all, looking after my pets was the one thing that kept me going.

From another perspective, these two cats were the only sense of responsibility I had at that moment in my life, and I couldn't just leave them. Their existence proved that I was actually able to look after something and do an OK job; without feeling as though I was burdened. Although an extremely subtle version of this emotion, being able to look after my cats did ignite a tiny spark of satisfaction.

Many pet owners will agree that our animals can help to lift our mood, especially when they play and do silly things. Our new cat getting stuck in strange places comes to mind, as does the way he makes me chuckle with the noises that emanate from his favourite basket. I strongly believe that the right pet can help create a more positive atmosphere, and gives us owners a reason to look forward to going home. My house wouldn't feel right without a cat or two wandering around looking for something to chew on, and they certainly take away that sense of emptiness and loneliness.

Quick Tip

- If you already own a pet, take a moment to appreciate them again. Often we co-exist in busy lives and forget to give them a bit of time. Sometimes focussing on an animal can give you less of a chance to become lost in depressive thoughts, and it is likely that they will relish the attention. One of my cats can never play fetch too many times, and this makes for an excellent distraction when I need to focus on something other than my negative thoughts. Don't assume that you need to have a pet you can stroke to make the most of this distraction either - other pets such as fish, can be very relaxing to watch.

- Dogs are a great excuse to get outside, and this in itself is a wonderful distraction. Next time you find yourself feeling in need; take the dog for a walk. Run, roll and play with him (or her) until you both come home wanting a nap. If you don't have a dog, perhaps you know someone who would appreciate you taking theirs out instead.

- Just as tidying and cleaning your home can work wonders for your mind, perhaps it is time to clean up around your pet? Don't allow yourself to put off changing the straw in Frodo's hutch, or the water in Nemo's tank. Maybe those food bowls could do with a wash, or a home found for the toys scattered around the living room. All of these things are extremely cathartic, and most likely need doing anyway. This is the perfect opportunity.

- It might sound one step closer to madness, but talking to a pet can be a great relief during times of despair. It will allow you the opportunity to talk without being judged, and you can go into as much, or little detail as you want; without the fear of being asked difficult questions. There have been many times in my life when Lancelot has cuddled up to me and listened to my sobs of anger or hurt, and I have found this to be very calming. Just having my cats around has helped me to appreciate companionship, and sometimes this has gently eased me into a frame of mind where I can turn my negative emotions around.

I can't necessarily explain the exact reason why stroking an animal can soothe and calm us; only agree that it certainly feels good to me. Whether it's a chemical reaction or emotional response; pets have been proven to relieve stress, and hence we should make the most of them. It's time to give that animal some fuss.

Sophia Gill

FREE

4 : UNTANGLE THE THREAD

When I was very little, my mum handed me various off-cuts of fabric plus a needle and thread, and then promptly taught me to sew. I passed the weekends making hair scrunchies that never stretched wide enough to fit before the seams bust open, beanbags full of strange smelling dried peas, and patchwork bags that threatened to spill their contents over the floor when you weren't looking. I continued to sew because I was quite happy knowing that I was simply able to transform those scraps, and therefore thought nothing more of it.

As the daughter of a seamstress you would think that as an adult I would at least know how to sew on a button, but somewhere between infant school and puberty, I simply lost the knack. It was only when my soon-to-be mother-in-law proudly showed me her wonderful sock animal creations, I fell in love with the marvel of what could be, and found inspiration to start sewing again.

Feeling depressed about my dead-end job and financial instability, I distracted myself from a month of hitting a roadblock in my writing by cutting up not my tired arms, but a pile of assorted socks. Suddenly those weren't just a cheap pack of plain black feet warmers for sale in Tesco's - they were the arms and legs of a slightly wonky, cute black cat, with legs as skinny as Mike. Sewing became a very new distraction to me, proving its worth with the promise of completely unique soft toys.

Concentrating on each stitch is a fantastic way to pass the time because you can literally see the product of your efforts forming before your very eyes.

Even small doses of satisfaction can help us to feel a sense of purpose and achievement; both of which are excellent emotions to battle depression.

It is also a great feeling to know that you *are* self-sufficient enough to mend things, even if your needlework isn't the tidiest out there. Let yourself be liberated by just being able to sew up that hole in your favourite jumper, or stitch back that button that's been missing for ages. Whereas this was common practice in previous generations, it is somewhat sad that we are now more likely to throw something away than try and fix it. Heaven forbid we actually do the work ourselves, yet it really it is such a satisfying hobby.

It is time for sewing to be back in fashion.

Quick Tip

- If your home is more likely to have a pile of damaged clothes than a sewing kit, go out and get yourself the basics. Sewing needles and thread don't have to be fancy, and you can pick them up for next to nothing.

- Rather than tackle your favourite shirt straight away, practice your handiwork by trying to make something simple; such as a stuffed toy or patchwork blanket. There are guides available online and in books, or perhaps someone you know wouldn't mind teaching you the basics. I was thrilled to finally learn how to tie a knot with a sewing needle! It doesn't matter how neat you are with each stitch; just that you are suitably distracted.

- There are other types of needlework, which are just as great, and some you might prefer to begin with. If sewing really isn't for you, why not give one or all of these a go: -

    o Crochet
    o Knitting
    o Quilting
    o Embroidery
    o Tapestry
    o Needlelace

- Remember that whichever of these you try, there are always two elements, both of which can be cheap and fun: -

  o   Mend something
  o   Create something new

- I personally prefer to indulge my artistic side by creating sock and glove creatures, but it is always in the back of my mind to finally mend the cat toy that got ripped in two, and reunite Mike's buttons with their former clothes.

- Have a look around your home and remind yourself of things that need a quick repair, or items that you've been meaning to buy. Perhaps you can make them instead! Whilst it might not be practical (or fashionable) to dump the shopping centres and handmake all your own clothes, there are still things that are perfect for this distraction. Toys are especially fun and easy to make, but you could also attempt to knit a scarf, sew a patchwork cushion (great for pets), embroid a work of art to hang on your wall, or tart up some plain napkins. All of these can also make great gifts; so let your imagination run wild.

Sophia Gill

FREE

5 : THE LIST OF ALL LISTS

When I decided to write this book, I already knew that it was destined to be so much more than just a simple list of things to do. The beauty of it had to lie in the way it connected with you, and inspired the want to get better - using these distractions to help. What I also learned during the process of creating 101 ideas was that basic list-making was also excellent and worthy of being its own chapter.

Whilst you might argue that lists are not the most important things in our lives, sometimes the act of making one can open our minds to ideas and thoughts; which help us along a more positive and constructive path. This is exactly why depression is such a bastard to conquer; it makes us lose all our ability to be constructive, and replaces it with this constant 'need' to destroy even a glimpse of something good. At my worst, I lost all sense of self-confidence and worth, and became only able to look at everything around me through muddy glasses. There were no roses in sight.

Constructive criticism was to me as mythical as the Holy Grail, for it translated in my mind as pure criticism. I had lost the tools to be able to 'deal' with anything, and subsequently even getting out of bed became a struggle. This wasn't just me being a lazy teenager; it was depression rendering me useless from the inside out.

So how can a list help?

When you write things down, those thoughts are staring back at you in black and white. Having things in writing helps to make them feel more concrete, and often this means we are more inspired to tackle any problems. Naturally, writing a list takes very little artistic skill, and so it is a lot less daunting that trying to write something more substantial. If you think about how satisfying it is to physically cross things off a 'to do' list, you'll know what I mean when I say that lists can give us a gentle push to be more productive - and feel good for it.

The question is, what to make a list of?

Quick Tip

- As you begin to recognise your soul-destroyer, you will find that there are certain signs that can warn you it is creeping up on you. It took me a while to clearly define my own, but when I began to write them down I found that I was much better at deciding when help was needed. As an example, I knew that when I started texting with very short but meaningful words, it was a sign I was beginning to slip. So too was depression consuming me when I listened to certain music, slept all day without being ill, and didn't eat despite being hungry. Your signs might be variants or mine, or they could be completely different. Recognising and putting these signs in a list is the first step to controlling your negative feelings, and understanding means that they cannot spiral out of control or attack without warning.

- One of my favourites is to write in one column the things that you think are good about yourself or situation, and then a list of the bad in another. You could even create a third column for your future hopes and dreams. The idea here isn't to nitpick, but to try and give you a better perspective. When you are feeling bad; take out the list and remind yourself of the good. When you are having a strong day; perhaps you can try to tackle one of the things in the 'bad' column. You may even change your mind about their existence, or find a way to deal with some of the problems constructively.

- Here are some other ideas: -

  o Make a list of the things that you would say to the 'depressed you'. Do you notice that your perspective on things change depending on your mood? Which 'voice' should you listen to?
  o Save yourself hours of traipsing through shops not knowing what to buy, by making a list of Christmas and/or birthday

presents that you'd like to get friends and family. This simple act can save time, money, and many frustrated hours - especially if you then cross items off the list by shopping online. The Internet eh - isn't it wonderful!

o Shopping lists always help us to steer our supermarket trolleys on track, and avoids filling them with junk food, and special offers we don't need. Next time you pop out for groceries, remember to make a list first.

o If you've ever found yourself just about to buy a film, and have stopped to ponder over whether or not you already have it; then maybe it is time to form a list of your collection of DVDs and/or Blu-rays. The same applies to music, and anything else that you might collect.

o How about a list to tell you what lists you have? One list to rule all lists, if you please!

Whatever you make a list of, never be afraid to cross things off it, add more, or completely start again. You are, of course, allowed to change your mind, so remember to allow yourself that freedom - especially if it means taking things out of the 'bad' column and adding new things to the 'good' one. My list of how I see myself is very different today from when I was really suffering with depression, and it is being able to reflect back that helped me to see that things were changing. Again, depression feels endless and without resolution, so having these lists can also be very helpful throughout your journey because they can act as points of reference during moments when everything seems blurry.

Sophia Gill

FREE

6 : ANSWER YOUR OWN QUESTIONS

Next time you find yourself thinking 'I wonder what it is like to..?' or 'Why is it that..?' jot the thought down. When the need for a distraction finds you, flick through those random thoughts and pick one to look into.

Life is full of questions, and for those of us who are interested; there are answers out there too. Some might be easy to find, others nearly impossible. This distraction is all about the hunt. Learning along the way is simply a bonus.

The beauty of this idea is that it is totally tailored to you, and can take up as much time as you want it to. It doesn't matter if you suspect your question might be silly - perhaps that's the very reason you've never asked it. With friends like Google, you need not be afraid of your own curiosity ever again.

Finding the answers gives you a great sense of achievement, and often leads you to ask more questions. You could call this a self-replenishing distraction! Your newly learned fact could be something you hold personal to you, or it could be something you take pleasure in sharing with others. It doesn't matter how you use the new information, the point is that instead of letting soul-destroyers consume you, you've bided your time productively until you've found the strength to fight back.

On days when I have found myself feeling fed up and miserable, I often find myself answering all kinds of seemingly pointless questions. In fact, just today I've spent hours trying to decide which reusable nappies I would recommend, and I don't even have, nor plan to have a baby.

My new knowledge of nappies has purely been spawn out of curiosity, and it is information that I shall most likely never discuss with anyone (otherwise they might start to look at my tummy differently) To an outsider this might sound like time wasted, but it's helped me get through another day without depression, and that, for me is enough.

Quick Tip

- Is there stuff you've always wondered about but never taken the time to research? Maybe you are trying to decide the best camera to take on holiday, or the best computer for your home? Or maybe there is a more general topic that you've always wondered about, like how old is a cat in human years? Take the time now to try and find answers. You could start on the Internet, or by looking in books and asking people.

- Here are some of my personal ponders - if you can't think of your own, why not try and find answers to mine?

  - Why does tea end up with froth on the top if you use water that hasn't quite fully boiled?
  - Are reusable nappies as good as disposables?
  - What is that song they use on that advert? (Which advert I hear you say? - you decide!)
  - How is it possible to predict the weather?

FREE

7 : DISTURB THE BED BUGS

Don't you just love that feeling when you first get into bed and the sheets are crisp, clean and fresh? When you pull the duvet up to your chin, and a waft of laundry detergent drifts over you. It's lovely isn't it! It doesn't matter how many times we seem to be changing the sheets in our house, it's never often enough.

Pulling the dirty linen off your bed and swapping them with fresh sheets and clean covers, is a surprisingly good distraction because not only is it something that you probably needed to do anyway -you will also be grateful of it later that evening when it's time to reap the reward.

Sleep is an important part of how you feel right now and how you will cope, so it is vital that your night-time environment is as good as it can be. If you are anything like me, a change of sheets isn't going to be the cure to a backlog of insomnia, but it can certainly make you feel just a little bit more comfortable.

Being somewhat of a perfectionist also helps make this distraction worthwhile, as it literally exhausts me. By the time our bed is done, I'm so hot and tired that I'm ready to get in it. Doing anything to exert energy is important especially when you are trying to break the addiction of self-harm, because it will help you to dispel some of that anger. I used to feel quite drained and calm after I had just cut myself, and so I recognised that this was the feeling I needed to replicate by other means in order to help me cope. This is another reason why exercise is such an important distraction; so don't overlook the ideas in this book which sound tiring.

Quick Tip

- Before you put new linen on your bed, remember to vacuum your mattress and also flip it over. This helps to clean any dust or dirt that will naturally build up in the mattress, and also helps extend the lifespan by moving the location of the wear.

- Whenever I put clean sheets on our bed, I also finish the job off with a couple of sprays of nice smelling sleep mist. I use the Molton Brown range, but there are sprays available from loads of other places, which smell just as nice. This also helps me sleep better, as I find the lavender very relaxing. If you don't already have something suitable, pop it on your shopping list now so that you can pick up some linen spray next time you are out (or shopping online).

- Perhaps it is time to treat yourself to some new bed sheets? If you're still putting covers on your bed that you bought when you left Uni, now is a good time to invest in some more. Likewise, you might find that a new duvet or pillow will help you feel more comfortable and thus sleep better.

FREE

8 : STEP INTO THE LIGHT

Anyone who has done even a tiny bit of research on Seasonal Affective Disorder can begin to understand how important the sun is to our mental wellbeing. Of course the lack of sunlight is not the reason depression exists, but anyone with a predisposition to the illness might find that increasing their time outside in natural light could help.

I'm not a scientist, and therefore can't explain the exact reason or process which links our happiness to the amount of natural light we are exposed to*, but I can tell you that locking yourself away in a dark room is not going to help rid yourself of those depressive feelings.

I always 'knew' that I belonged in a sunnier climate; not just because I was born of a Latino disposition, but because I feel as though I have this in-built desire to get outside. Mike will tell you how fidgety I get if we find ourselves spending a weekend indoors. I become short-tempered and frustrated, and start despising modern inventions such as televisions and computers. I don't think of myself as depressed anymore, but it is as if I simply 'know' that it would all too easily take over my life again if I even give it an inch.

Spending time in the sun has become part of my routine to help level my mood and give me mental clarity, and I genuinely think it is an important part of your own recovery. Many of the distractions in this book mean going outside, and so you have no excuse to keep yourself hostage indoors any longer.

Quick Tip

- No matter what you decide to do, get yourself outside. Natural light is so important to our physical wellbeing that I truly believe you can't have too much of it. Of course if the sun in blazing and you are at a risk of burning; limit the time you spend in direct sunlight and ensure you protect your skin with sun lotion and clothing.

- Try and introduce periods of outdoor time into your daily routine. Perhaps you can walk to work or the shops instead of being cooped up in a car, bus or train? If you usually spend your lunch breaks sat at your desk, why not sit outside for that time instead. It doesn't matter if your surroundings aren't perfect; this is all about giving your body a chance to simply be in natural light. Best of all, you can do this sitting totally still. (Although exercising outside has added benefits.)

- Even if it is cloudy or dark right now, your body will still thank you for the fresh air; and this is another reason why being outside is so important. Many of us spend a large percentage of our time either in stuffy office buildings, air-conditioned shops and cars, or relaxing in our homes with the windows and curtains shut. Fresh air encourages us to think with better clarity, and this itself can dramatically change our mood. My experience with depression was that it was like a thick fog; twisting and misshaping my thoughts so that I always saw the bad in everything. Anything that can be used as a tool to combat this ambiguity is without a doubt, worth trying.

- It might be worth considering investing in a light box that you sit in front of for periods of time; especially during darker seasons. It has to be said that these are fairly expensive however, but at very least you could perhaps try a bulb that produces full-spectrum light. We have one in our bedroom for times when it's grey outside, and it is a much brighter and 'cleaner' light than a standard bulb. (A high-Watt bulb isn't the same.)

- To try and help with Circadian rhythms (a natural pattern that our bodies follow during the day) we have an alarm clock that mimics sunrise. This really does help me get to sleep and wake better, and I can definitely recommend them; especially if your bedroom is still fairly dark in the mornings.

*It might help if you think of it this way. The human body was designed to spend frequent amounts of time outside. This is how we evolved, and our bodies are quite capable of turning sun exposure into valuable nutrients. It is simply not natural for our bodies to spend so much time inside, and what affects the physical being will invariably affect the mind.

The levels of serotonin and melatonin in our bodies are changed by how much sunlight we get, and low levels of serotonin; caused by high levels of melatonin, creates feelings of depression. It is therefore understandable that exposure to light; which lowers the melatonin levels, has the reverse effect: thus elevating our mood.

Sophia Gill

FREE

9 : CHANGE THAT CD

Music has the ability to be so powerful, and yet sometimes we don't even notice the effect it has on us. Imagine watching a classic romantic film with all the music taken out. Think of that poignant moment when our hero proposes to his long lost love. Without music, it's probably going to seem like two people having an ordinary chat together. The long and drawn-out silence before she says 'yes' is probably going to be just that: long and drawn-out. The music is carefully chosen because it helps us viewers get 'lost' in the film. Just as music can add to an atmosphere, I am always amazed by just how much it is able to change or create it too.

When I used to come home angry and depressed, I would instinctively put on music that related to how I was feeling. Before long, I would find myself in the 'self-harm zone', feeling powerless to get out without cutting. The songs I had chosen had strengthened the depression so much, that just hearing one of my 'self-harm songs'; even when I was feeling happy, would reduce me to tears.

The problem is, I thought that these songs made me feel less alone; like the artist understood my pain and suffering. Whilst this might have an element of truth, the important fact is that my music was not helping me. I found it incredibly hard not to listen to certain types of music when I was in certain types of moods, but when I did finally make that switch; I became able to manipulate my emotions with a simple song. Suddenly depression found it harder to consume me, and that is when I started winning the battle.

Quick Tip

- Make a playlist of songs that uplift you. Songs that make you jiggle your feet and want to sing along. If a song makes you smile, then it gets added to the list. You'll find no tearjerkers here thank you! Arm yourself with the collection, and use it to fight away the bad times.

- If you haven't got around to making your uplifting playlist yet, at very least you should fight those urges to put on depressing songs when you are already feeling a bit down. I know that you are drawn to them, but you must understand that their attraction is only indulging depression's need to wallow. Deny yourself this, and you will quickly discover that positive thoughts don't come from music that makes you want to slit your wrists. Trust me when I say this; much of my self-harm could have been avoided if I had simply changed that CD. It is better to listen to nothing at all (see distraction number 56) than to let music trigger more negative feelings.

- Perhaps you could get in touch with your creative side and try to make some music. You could do this either digitally by the wonders of modern technology, or perhaps by using real instruments. (See distraction number 90.) If you've never been great with that guitar, why have a go singing. (see distraction number 34) or try and write song lyrics.

FREE TO 🐷

10 : DAMN, WHAT IS THAT WORD?

I not long ago discovered that crosswords, word searches, Sudoku, and similar puzzles are surprisingly effective distractions, and are extremely easy to get into. There are always puzzle books for sale in newsagents, and many come free with newspapers. You don't even need paper copies anymore, as many puzzles can be done online.

When I was having some problems at work and had started cutting myself again, it was very hard to drop everything and get help when I was meant to be at my desk working. I found it so much easier to slope off in my lunch break and cut my arms with a pocket-knife, but deep down knew that this was not an addiction I wanted to go back to. Although it was extremely difficult to resist this urge, I can honestly say that when I forced myself to instead focus my energy on the puzzle book sat on my desk, I did sometimes manage to end the day without fresh cuts. Sometimes is better than no times, and hence why this might just be the distraction that works for you.

Quick Tip

- Next time you are passing a newsagent, pick up a puzzle book to keep at your desk or in your bag. I preferred to buy the ones that contained a variety of puzzles, but you can also buy books that only have a certain type in them. You will soon learn which ones you enjoy the most. They are cheap, and never go out of date, and the puzzles vary in difficulty so it doesn't matter if you're only just beginning. Try and keep this book with you at times when you know you might need a distraction. If you do end up finishing most of the puzzles, or reach the pages where they are getting too hard, bin it and buy another.

- If you need a distraction right now but haven't had a chance to get yourself a puzzle book, have a look online for some. The great thing about the Internet is that it's always there when you need it, but it does help to have a specific use for the World Wide Web - else you could find yourself wandering aimlessly for days.

FREE

11 : SAVE THE PLANET

The fact that we are all destroying our planet is not new news, but it is quite common to feel like there is little we can do to help. But there is! Not only will doing things to save the planet help towards a greater cause, they can double up as damn good distractions.

I went through a bit of a phase where I ignored depression and instead focussed my efforts into making our home better for the environment (and our bills). Naturally anything to drag me away from my usual thoughts was a bonus, but I also learned that there was something very satisfying about knowing you are doing your bit to help the planet. It might not seem like much (what difference can I make anyway?) but you have to believe that your effort does count. After all, if everyone took the attitude that their input was a waste, then nothing would ever get done. Even if you find it all hard to believe, why not try this distraction anyway?

Have a think about ways you could be more 'green'. Go around your house and make notes if you think that would be easier. Whilst it is not always practical to be as eco-friendly as we perhaps could be, often there are simple changes that we can make, which benefit the environment. Although it might take a bit more planning and effort to put your changes into practice, having a look at your life to see where those changes can be made is something that you can do whatever time of day or night it is right now.

Quick Tip

- Here are some questions to think about, hopefully helping you find ideas to live a more eco-friendly life: -

  o Are you recycling enough? Are there times you don't recycle when you perhaps could?

  o Could you add a water saver to your toilets, so that it uses less water when you flush?

  o Is it possible to fit a rain collector in your garden? - You could use the collected rain to water plants.

  o Are there plugs you never turn off, or is your television left in standby? - Not only does this waste electricity, but you are also paying for it in your bills.

  o Could your heating be more efficient?

  o Is there a pile of paperwork that could be recycled instead of put in the bin?

  o Are you already separating food waste so that it can be composted? Could you compost at home?

  o Is your baby still in nappies? - Perhaps you can give re-usable nappies a try. They've come a long way since the terry cloth days (or so I'm told) and can really save you money in the long run.

- I would also suggest taking a look online for other ideas on how to make your home more eco-friendly, as new energy-saving gadgets and the like, are being launched all the time.

FREE

12 : GET CAUGHT IN THE WEB

Ah the Internet! Although I wasn't born while dinosaurs roamed the Earth, the Internet; believe it or not, wasn't widely available when depression had its hooks into me. Hard to imagine a world without the net now though isn't it?

I.T. issues aside, the Internet can be both a blessing in disguise and a wolf in sheep's clothing. However, in moderation it can be a wonderful distraction.

I know for a fact that I would have benefitted from having net access when I was at my worst, for two very important reasons. Firstly, with a tiny amount of searching online I would have discovered that I most certainly was not alone with what I was going through. Nowadays it is possible to find support groups for almost anything, and I know that the self-harm forums would have given me some comfort during those times when I felt so terribly alone. Secondly, I believe that understanding is the key to recovery. If you can understand what it is that you need to find a distraction from, you will be better equipped to keep those negative thoughts at bay. Again, there is enough information online to at least help you start to understand.

A word of warning however - sometimes reading forums about self-harm and depression at a time when I was feeling particularly vulnerable often made me worse. Although that might just be my experience, it is important to recognise whether or not what you choose to do online is helping or hindering your emotions.

Quick Tip

- Why not use the Internet to: -

  o   Research a hobby or interest.
  o   Read the news.
  o   Write reviews on things you have or have done.
  o   Read reviews on stuff you are interested in.
  o   Browse all the strange things for sale on ebay (but don't get caught up buying too much).
  o   Search for jokes, amusing pictures or cartoons.
  o   Perhaps look for a new job.
  o   Catch up with your friends on social networking websites.

My personal favourite is to waste away time that would otherwise be spent feeling miserable, by researching all the special offers I can find. From flights for £1 to hotels for £10, I am in my element when I am booking mini adventures for less than the cost of our broadband access.

FREE TO

13 : PANCAKE DAY TODAY

There is something about making pancakes that makes me feel like I'm an excited, carefree child again - begging my sister to let me have the next one. It doesn't matter how rubbish my day has been. As soon as I start mixing the batter and preparing my toppings of choice, I'm instantly happy. It's these small pleasures in life that are the first to be obscured by depression's grey cloud, hence why re-discovering them is a subtle grasp onto normality. Why should we limit pancakes to Shrove Tuesday? Every day should be a pancake day!

The great thing about pancakes is that they are very easy to cook and are extremely yummy. The batter mix is simple to make from scratch, but even if that is too much to think about, you can buy ready-made pancake mixes that cost next to nothing. (My favourite is the supermarket-own brand batter mix for 10p.) These packs last for ages; meaning you can store them in the cupboard ready for when you spontaneously decide that pancakes are what's been missing from your day. Part of their beauty lies in the simplicity: pancakes require only minimal effort but produce a great reward. Even if I felt too depressed to think about food, I was still able to muster the energy to beat an egg and water together with a packet of batter mix.

The only difficulty I face with pancakes is knowing when I've had enough. I've often gone to bed feeling a little bit sick because I wanted 'just one more'. Remember you don't *have* to use up all the batter: why not share them with your friends or family, or save some for the following day instead?

Quick Tip

- If you've already mastered the art of making pancakes, why not: -

    o Experiment with fillings. I've tried mushroom and cheese, but my favourite is still the classic lemon and sugar.
    o See if you can toss them (cleaning up afterwards can be another distraction!)
    o Try and make specially shaped pancakes. Can you make one that looks like a heart, or perhaps in the shape of a country? (No cheating with moulds or pastry cutters here)
    o If you normally fold them, try eating them rolled, or vice versa. Do they taste different if you eat them with a knife and fork instead of with fingers?

FREE

14 : THE TIME FACTOR

This is perhaps one of the more difficult distractions in this book, despite it sounding very obvious and basic. It is born of the idea to 'sleep on it' - a cliché that is often applicable in our lives. The idea behind 'the time factor' is to do one or both of the following two things: -

One

The first is to simply wait a set amount of time before doing something. How long that wait should be is up to you, but you should at very least allow it to be long enough for your mind to regain some space. Set yourself a smaller goal to start with; such as five or ten minutes, then perhaps increase it over time.

If you first set this to a short amount such as five minutes, and after that wait you feel no change at all; try increasing it to ten minutes. Slowly raise the amount up and up until you notice that you feel slightly different before and after. This is how you will discover the length of time needed for you; as it will invariably be different for everyone, and every situation. The actual waiting part should feel difficult and possibly frustrating, but this no doubt means that it is working.

The idea here is that if right now you are feeling angry, upset or stressed, if there is any decision to be made you are likely to make the wrong one. Negative emotions always get in the way at times like this, and this can make even the most logical person say or do something irrational. We all have times where we snap, but often this leads to feeling regret and embarrassment later on.

Instead of immediately taking action; which could mean self-harm for some people, firmly wait for you pre-determined time to pass. Reassess the situation, and your feelings afterwards, and you might be surprised to find that your outlook, and thus the outcome has changed. It might be a very subtle difference, and perhaps doesn't change the decision you had already made previously, but at very least it gives you the opportunity to let those emotions run their course so that your mind can think more clearly. You can also enter the decision knowing it wasn't made on the spur of the moment; which helps you maintain the strength of your convictions.

Two

The second part of this distraction is to only do something for set amount of time. This is perhaps even harder than waiting before you do something, but can be equally as beneficial. The only time I would suggest that this distraction is not applicable, is if we are doing something that is fun and making us feel better (but then that would render this whole book useless, right?!)

Similarly to part one, decide on a fixed amount of time that you will 'allow' yourself to indulge these feelings, and be strict on yourself to stick to it. The perfect example here is if right now you feel completely miserable and lost, and just want to cry. Waiting ten minutes or so probably won't change that feeling, and so you could think of part two as a 'backup plan.' Tell yourself you will cry for only five minutes (or whatever time you feel is suitable for you) then allow yourself to express those emotions. Setting a time limit on them stops you from dwelling for too long, and could perhaps help you to move on.

I know for a fact that I am very strict on myself, yet when it comes to depression, misery completely takes over and can render me useless for days. This is not only difficult and unhealthy; it is impractical. Most of us have commitments such as work and family, and crying non-stop for days is only going to strengthen any feelings of guilt. Obviously it is important to allow certain thoughts to pass naturally, but certainly there are also times when dwelling truly doesn't help.

It might sound very regimental and clinical to put time limits on our feelings, but I honestly believe that anything that can help us compartmentalize negative emotions helps us to understand and cope with them.

Quick Tip

- Decide now on your time limit both to wait and to do, and try as hard as you can to stick to them. Increase the time as you feel necessary, but do it in small stages so it is manageable.

- If you are struggling to wait for your set period, try and fight it out even if this means pacing around the room or speaking to a friend. This might be the perfect time to slot in one of the other distractions from this book; such as walking (see distraction number 61), using the Internet (see distraction number 12), or any of the others in the short-term section. The goal is to change how you feel during this time, but don't be too hard on yourself if the change is minor, or not at all.

- Stopping yourself from dwelling is extremely hard, so try and set yourself something to do once your set period of time has passed. For example, 'I'll allow myself to feel sorry for myself for twenty minutes, then afterwards I shall have a cup of tea and start preparing dinner.'

- Parts one and two can de done in any order, independently or together, so don't feel as though you have to stick to this exact format. For some occasions waiting is right, and other times it is restricting the time that is more important. Try and test both until you can better understand which one to use and when.

Sophia Gill

FREE TO

15 : EPISODE BY EPISODE

This is hands down, one of my favourite, easy, short-term distractions. I still use it so regularly that for a while I even forgot to include it in the book. It is such an obvious idea that I simply took it for granted.

There are not many people in the world who can proclaim to not have access to a television, and increasingly common is the household DVD player. They are cheap, easily available, and simple to use. Even most computers have DVD players by default now, and the cost of the discs themselves is coming down dramatically, especially since the advent of Blu-ray. This all paves way to the perfect distraction.

Watching a television series during times like this is great because they require much less commitment than a film. I tended to find myself feeling those self-harm urges late at night, yet I was too conscious of my sleep needs to distract myself with a full movie. Feeling depressed was one thing, but feeling depressed and tired was really asking for trouble!

Very little effort is required to plonk yourself down on the sofa, or to wiggle yourself comfortable in bed, and this is another reason why this distraction can be so appealing. Even your soul-destroyer will be hard-pushed to convince you of a reason not try it.

The other thing I love about TV series' is that they are often complete stories; wrapped up in less than an hour. When you really 'get into' a series, you are engaged with the characters and plot so much, that for this short period you can think of nothing else. If it's the type of show to leave you hanging, you'll be craving the next one so much that, again, you might find yourself temporarily forgetting about those problems.

This is exactly what this book of distractions is all about. I actually noticed that much of the solution to my self-harm addiction was piecing together small distractions so that my mind had enough time to figure out how to help myself. In fact, many of the distractions were my actual help; such as writing, and so trying these ideas gave me the opportunity to find out which ones worked for me.

Personally, I prefer to watch television series' on DVD, simply because it means I have them to hand when I need them, and I don't have to patiently wait another week for the next episode to be broadcast. Whilst either will work, having them on DVD seems more logically suitable to this cause, and so I would encourage you to invest in at least one box set.

Quick Tip

- If it's getting quite late in the evening, and you just need a distraction that won't mean you are shattered for work the next day, TV series' are perfect. Perhaps you already have one on DVD that you could watch again, or maybe the next season is out, ready to add to your collection.

- If you've been following your favourite series and are keen to find something similar, take a look at reviews online and see what other people recommend. I've discovered loads of great programs by doing this, and the list of want-to-watch series' is ever-growing.

- Although I rarely do this myself, simply watching television can be a good distraction also, and this might suit your circumstances right now. Remember to try and pick something that will fully involve you. There is no point turning on the TV if it will just act as background noise to your negative thoughts.

FREE (IF YOU HAVE A BIKE)

TO

16 : DON THE CYCLING SHORTS

I can't actually remember what or who inspired me to buy a bicycle. It was probably one of my spontaneous attempts at 'fixing' my mood by spending money I didn't have. When I did it, I certainly did it with style. Almost £500 later, and there I was in horrible old lycra shorts and mismatched tee-shirt, pushing my shiny bike across the road to the park (because I was too scared to actually cycle it there). Now what happened next is very cliché, but until you try it you just won't quite get how true this is.

The wind blew through my hair. The sun shone down on my back. I whooshed past the odd dog-walker like I was the only person who mattered, and the deer smiled nervously as I wobbled slowly past them. The sound of my pedals going round and around echoed through my mind, lulling me into a deep sense of satisfaction. It felt wonderful. I thought I could go for miles. I was carefree, and I was free.

Cheese aside, what matters is that it successfully took my mind off things. So I probably should have paced myself a little because the next day I could hardly walk, but even through a pained limp, I had a spring in my step. I'd come home relieved of my pent-up anger and frustration, feeling healthy and exhausted. I slept better, I didn't crave junk food, and I was more energetic. Damn it! Exercise DOES make you feel better! Everyone had been saying this to me for years and although I appreciated they were probably right, I didn't realise just what a difference it would make.

Quick Tip

- Brush off the crusted mud and dead spiders, and get yourself out on your bike. If you haven't got one, is there anyone you know who might lend you theirs? Or perhaps you can set yourself a budget and put some money aside to invest in your own pair of wheels. You don't have to spend much on a bike - I just got greedy when I chose mine.

- Perhaps you have an exercise bike that hasn't had as much use as you first intended it to? I bought mine with great expectations, but quickly realised that sitting on the sofa with a packet of Wotsits was so much easier. I recently dusted it off and set myself a goal of peddling two miles at least every other day, in the hope that my wedding dress would still fit me for the big day next year. The rhythmic sound of the pedals going around and around is very hypnotic and soothing, and I feel extremely chuffed with myself when the numbers on that dial finally say '2.00'.

FREE

17 : PHONE A FRIEND

As mentioned in distraction 76, often we find ourselves being consumed by misery for the simple reason that we are feeling completely alone. With the modern age pushing us further into our computers and away from 'real' communication, it is all too easy to forget that actually speaking to someone can make a massive difference.

In a rather hypocritical fashion, phoning my friends in a moment of need was always something that I was terrible at doing. I used to feel that I was a burden; a waste of time and a pain in the bum. It didn't matter how many times they told me 'we would rather you phoned us in the middle of the night than cut yourself,' I always struggled to dial those numbers.

It's not even that I didn't have friends who I felt I could really open up to and trust completely. Both Rue and Scott were always patient, calm and strong for me, yet I still felt as though I was being a pest.

What I didn't see until now however, is that this instinct to retreat into my lonely cave was just another of depression's tricks. True friends don't feel burdened by your low points, just as you don't by theirs. If anything, I was hurting my friends more by denying them a chance to help, than the imaginary pain I thought I would cause them by putting a downer on their evening with my teary phone call.

If this was a game of 'who wants to be a self-harmer tonight?' it would be no good asking the audience - what do they know anyway; they are just a bunch of strangers. 50:50 won't help either because this leaves you just as confused as when you started. No - the best option here is to pluck up the courage and phone a friend.

Quick Tip

- Ignore those voices in your mind telling you that people don't care. They do; and would rather hear from you now than find out about this later. Pick up your phone and call them. Texting, emailing or instant messaging just isn't the same, and in times like this, real progression is made only when speaking.

- Don't be disheartened if the friend you call doesn't answer. Ignore depression when it tells you 'they are ignoring you, they hate you' - it is more likely that this person is out, on the toilet, or honestly didn't hear the phone ring. Simply call someone else.

- I do appreciate that I have been very lucky with people I have made friends with, and that not everyone has someone they feel they can talk to. If you are nodding in agreement, this distraction can still work for you. Try calling one of the crisis hotlines available, such as SANEline or ChildLine. I have spoken to a couple of different ones in real moments of despair; one time being when I had tried to commit suicide. The volunteers who answer the calls can be fantastic to speak to, and in my opinion, talking to someone who is trained to listen is much better than staying alone.

I've always said that the people who didn't understand self-harm or depression were the people who I didn't want in my life anyway, and this has actually been an excellent litmus test for finding true friendship. No doubt you already know who your real friends are anyway, but if someone does react badly to your phone call, perhaps it is time to re-evaluate your connections. It might sound harsh, but it is perfectly natural to lose old friends and make new ones throughout life.

FREE

18 : IN IT TO WIN IT

Competitions can be a great distraction from the mundane feeling that life tends to dish out. While it's best not to get too caught up with the 'what ifs' associated with money, there are plenty of competitions that can fill the gaps of depressive boredom nicely.

During one particularly uninteresting afternoon, I found myself navigating to an online DIY shop in the hunt for a perfectly cheap, yet sturdy shed. Instead, I found a writing competition to win one. I couldn't believe my luck. It was as if it had been created just for me; I loved writing, I was broke, and I really, really needed a shed.

I got to work on my story straight away, and before I knew it, my boring day had been and gone and it was the long-awaited weekend already. That Saturday I realised that my competitive streak had been unleashed on the world, and with sheer determination, I convinced Mike that we should make a video entry. Our sunny, otherwise empty weekend was quickly filled with photography, puppets, sound engineering and editing, to produce a wonderful animation; which was quite frankly too good for a simple competition. 'DIY Fred' was proudly uploaded to YouTube, while I sat back and noticed that I had been successfully distracted for almost two full days.

Quick Tip

- Don't think too much about what you would do if you won millions - the fall back down to earth after realising you haven't won the lottery can be quite depressing. There are all kinds of competitions running at most points in time, from crosswords, to writing, to ones where you simply send in your name and contact details to enter. Have a look online for ones that might be of interest, or perhaps flick through your favourite magazine. People also post details on forums, often with clues to the correct answer.

- To feel that buzz of satisfaction, look to enter competitions that incite your creativity. You might need to write a story or poem, take a photo, or perhaps make something. When you find yourself proud of something you have created, the actual winning part becomes insignificant.

Even if the prize doesn't interest you, if a competition gets you out there channelling your energy, then enter it. I've submitted work to writing competitions purely on the basis that it was a chance to distract from writing this very book (ironic I know) and focus on something that didn't mean quite so much to me. It was my own way of taking the pressure off, and if I won something in the meantime, then great. I could always give the prize away.

FREE TO 🐷

19 : SPIN THE GLOBE

As much as I believe that it is an important part of life to experience other parts of the world, for most of us it is neither practical nor affordable to throw everything into a suitcase and jet off into the clouds.

Travelling is naturally in this book, as long-term distraction number 101, but here you will find a much easier idea about simply admiring the world on an actual globe.

Somebody once bought me an inflatable beach ball style globe - complete with a plastic stand, and it bounced around my room for some years before finally deflating itself. Although not a very permanent addition to my collection of things, I remember how fascinating this globe was to look at. Much of the time I remember about my years with depression was about finding other things to do so that this illness did not overwhelm me. Spending time looking at a globe is obviously educational, but it can also be peaceful and inspiring. I would find myself feeling curious by the various location names, and thinking to myself 'I never realised that country was next to, or as big as..' Time would pass without glances at my watch, and I would be left with a strangely satisfied feeling: as though I was somehow bettering myself.

Naturally any form of learning that we do helps fight soul-destroyers such as depression, because it results in us knowing that we have more to offer in life; more of a purpose. This is an extremely powerful weapon against negative emotions, and even the slightest knowledge that we acquire can act as ammunition.

I believe that learning about the world in any way shape or form, not only makes us more interesting, but also helps us to have empathy for others. Whilst a globe alone is not going to change the way you understand another country, it might start off a chain of thoughts about how things are elsewhere in the world.

Quick Tip

- If you don't already have a globe and can't think of a place to store something so round, why not try and find an inflatable one like I had, or perhaps a simple atlas. This doesn't have to be an expensive purchase, and you can just as easily make it free by looking at maps online.

- Why not look up the different flags for various countries. You can find these online, or sometimes they are included in an atlas. Do the flags represent the country well? Are they interesting, boring, or unusual? Is the flag for that country how you expected it to look? Perhaps you can find out the meaning behind the design.

- As you look at your globe, atlas, or maps, try and ask yourself questions and think carefully about each answer. How close is each country to the equator? How would it feel to live in that kind of climate? How different would your life be if you lived there? Where would you go on holiday? Is that country rich or poor? Which languages do the people there speak? These are the kinds of questions I would naturally find myself pondering, and can help you to appreciate this simple, yet effective distraction.

FREE

20 : PRACTICE YOUR POKER FACE

Whenever I see someone playing cards, I always find myself wondering 'why didn't I think of that?' A game of cards is an excellent way to take your mind off things because just like distraction number 38, it forces you to concentrate on something very specific. Cards also have the added bonus of being very small and portable; so should be something that we can do anywhere, at any time.

Games offer us an incentive to play and generate a sense of fun (otherwise it'd be a pretty poor design) - and this is exactly why they work as brilliant distractions from depression. It is important to keep reminding ourselves of the pleasures in life, and this is something games are very good at.

Quick Tip

- Dig out that dusty old pack of cards, and remind yourself how to play a game or two. If you don't have anyone to play with right now, then enjoy a game of Solitaire. There are probably quite a few other games you could learn, so have a look at rules and tips online if you need some inspiration.

- In line with distraction 92, why not try and teach yourself some card tricks.

- If you don't have a pack of cards to hand, most computers have at least a game of Solitaire built into the operating system. Otherwise you could easily find somewhere to play card games online.

Caution

Don't get tempted to start playing cards on gambling sites or in casinos (or the like) - this is merely a suggestion of a simple distraction; not an offer to give up one addiction by taking on another!

When our minds are telling us that we have no enjoyment in life and that we'd be better off dead, we need to fight back by proving to ourselves that these paranoid delusions are exactly that: false figments of our depressive imagination. We all have hobbies and interests. Some of us may have either forgotten about them completely, or simply haven't discovered them yet.

If ever you find yourself convinced that nothing makes you happy and you are struggling to believe that the opposite is true; force yourself to at very least remember that no one can predict the future. Without knowing what lies ahead, we simply cannot deny the fact that something positive could be just around the corner. You may even find it in this book! It is a slow process I admit, but one that has to start with these small steps.

FREE

21 : GET CREATIVE

I have always believed that it is important to introduce an element of creativity in our lives, because the sense of achievement that we feel is unlike anything that can be replicated by other means.

My parents and older sister always encouraged me to make thinks when I was little, but as an adult I always struggle to find the time. It's a shame really. I always surprise myself when I put my mind to it, yet there is always something more urgent that needs doing.

This Christmas I deliberately bought cards that needed colouring in, and as predicted, it was the night before Christmas before we finally got around to doing them. Although we started colouring through a sense of obligation, it only took the first pencil to touch the paper for me to realise how therapeutic colouring was. If only someone had given me the idea when I was battling self-harm!

I remember that my child psychiatrist would always ask about the giant art folder that I carried to our Friday afternoon sessions; encouraging me to show him some of my work. It is only with Hindsight that I realise why he did so, and that it wasn't because he was interested to see what 15-year-olds did at school. Those show-and-tell sessions reminded me that my life wasn't all about the face of depression, and that I had skills and interests of my own.

It is only by taking the plunge to try and be creative, that you will realise those hidden talents; and this has the potential to keep you acquainted with the positives.

Quick Tip

The beauty of creativity is that it can emerge from many channels. You might not find colouring in very challenging or therapeutic, but perhaps one of these will inspire you: -

- Painting - Whether you paint by numbers in watercolours, or create giant canvasses with oil paints, painting also takes on many forms of its own. Try different mediums until you find one that you are comfortable with, and remember that you don't always have to paint on paper or canvas. (See distraction number 77.)

- Drawing - Remember that it doesn't matter how good at art you are to begin with; everyone needs time to improve. It will take some practice to find a style that you excel in, whether it be drawing cartoons, copying existing pictures, or sketching still life. Simply try putting pencil to paper with whatever comes to mind. Experiment with different grades of pencil, and also with colours.

- Make your own cards - Most of us will give a card to someone at some point in time. It might be to wish a happy birthday, or simply to let a person know we care. I've always kept a box full of odd cards that I've seen and bought, but you could take that a step further and hand-make some. It doesn't matter if you are not sure who it'll be for yet; just giving yourself a creative project can be an excellent distraction, which you can do at any time of day or night.

- Origami - Ah! The art of folding paper. I have to admit that I was quite keen on folding tiny bits of coloured paper into various farmyard animals. It takes a great amount of concentration to do, and just as you think your bit of paper couldn't look any less like the final product, a little tug here and a push there - and presto! A giraffe! It is perhaps best to start this distraction by following a guide of sorts, and my advice here is to follow that guide carefully.

- Make a model - This doesn't just have to mean digging out that stale Fimo collection. Perhaps you could try and create something out of wood or clay. This could even be linked to distraction number 87, whereby you could set yourself the task to make props, scenery or puppets.

There are so many other ways to be creative, and it is worth trying each one to see which you like best. For some other ideas, take a look at distraction numbers 2, 4, 24, 26, 29 or 46.

Sophia Gill

FREE

22 : TALK IT OUT

As shy as I used to be, I must admit that talking really helped me to combat depression. I may not have wanted to do it, and I may have spent many stubborn hours in total silence, but when I finally learned to open up there was no stopping me.

I consider myself very lucky to have been 'in the system' from very early on. Aged 14; and within my first year of self-harm, I took an overdose then panicked and rang ChildLine. Naturally they kept me on the phone and sent an ambulance round, but most importantly; I was forced into seeking regular help once leaving hospital.

My psychiatrist saw me almost immediately after the overdose and right up until the age when I was declared an adult. Whilst I may not have truly seen the point at the time; especially during those sessions when silence surrounded us for the full hour, I have come to realise that professional help was a big part of my healing process.

Having someone* to talk to: who wouldn't judge, criticise, laugh, scowl or shrink away in fear, was something that I did perhaps take for granted. However, I have come to appreciate just how vital communication is.

The beauty of talking is that it doesn't necessarily mean that only a Psychiatrist will be able to help you. From my own experience I would certainly suggest that you do try and seek professional help, but I also appreciate that it is not always possible, or even beneficial. Many of my friends found it extremely difficult to talk to their doctors, so I guess this does partially come down to luck of the draw.

Quick Tip

- First and foremost, only you can truly know if you are at a stage where you do need professional help. (A good clue is if the people you trust start to mention it.) If so, speak to you doctor and try and get referred to your local Psychiatric team. There may be a long waiting list, but it is worth a shot. If your doctor isn't very understanding; see another one. The same applies if you find it tricky to talk to the person you have been referred to. Everyone is different and we all get along with people in different ways. Trust is the key, and if this is missing you will find it very difficult to open up.

- Whilst waiting for a referral - or if you don't feel a Psychiatrist is right for you, never underestimate the value of talking to friends or family. True friends won't mind if you end up repeating yourself or showering them in tears, and you must ignore those thoughts making you feel as though you are a burden. Often this is just depression trying to isolate you, and you have to fight back by doing the opposite. (See distraction number 76.) Also don't be afraid to pick up the phone and call someone in your time of need. (See distraction number 17.) Generally people close to us react very well from being woken up once they realise the important step you have made by asking for help. This is especially true for those of us who are able to make a call instead of self-harming.

- It might sound one step closer to the nutty house, but talking to yourself can actually be very therapeutic. I'm not implying that you should replace all human contact with mirrors, but saying things out loud to yourself can certainly help you to churn things over. Just as reading aloud can make it much easier to spot mistakes in our writing, sometimes talking to no one in particular can dispel some of that anger and hurt; giving you a chance to welcome in the calm.

It has to be said that talking things over can help you see things with clarity, no matter whom you are actually speaking to. Mike and I have spent many hours discussing this very book, and those conversations have really helped me to better see the direction I was going in. Talking has given me ideas so quickly that I've barely had a chance to write them down before they are gone again, and almost certainly helped me to improve my writing style. Overall, this is one distraction that I cannot recommend enough.

*If you are on the receiving end of a conversation with a loved one, the best piece of advice I can give in relation to self-harm is to try not to focus too much on the cuts. From personal experience, when all I was being asked about was my self-harm, I began to lose a real sense of who I was. It was as though my life had become all about the damage I was doing to my body, and indirectly this made it harder to give up the addiction. It is a dangerous shift in focus and I cannot emphasise enough how important it is to keep the balance between showing that you care, but also moving towards the positives.

Also try and resist the temptation to link their self-harm to guilt by words such as 'if you really loved me you would stop cutting.' These are dangerous emotions to play with, and should never be bargained with. Sadly it is not as simple as loving someone enough to quit, and the guilt will be more damaging in the long run. Instead, try to help them encapsulate self-harm, so that it isn't linked to anything positive. This will make the addiction much easier to overcome.

Sophia Gill

FREE

23 : UNTIL IT SHINES

It is no secret that depression runs in my family. In some ways it has brought my dad and I closer together, as I've slowly learned that I can tell him things and find that he actually does understand. Fifteen years ago I wouldn't have even opened the door when he dropped by unannounced, yet now I am able to bounce ideas off him for a book I'm trying to write. Yes, my dad and I have come a long way.

It is only fair then, to credit my dad for the story of how polishing a brass car part helped him to trap his depression underneath an unfinished antique automobile. On days when he could barely find the strength of mind to speak, he would slink down to his workshop and spend hours rubbing down that brass. It was an act that took his mind off everything else that was going on, and gave my dad something to feel proud of for each little section that shone back.

Rubbing down that hunk of metal acted as the perfect distraction because it showed immediate results. With each circular movement of the hand, the original colours shined through. Whilst this might not sound especially satisfying to read about, it is most definitely something that has to be seen before you can fully appreciate it.

Quick Tip

- Whilst not many of us have bits of cars lying around, there are other things that can be polished with the same effect. Why not try polishing: -

- o Shoes - Give them a new lease of life.
- o Windows - It's probably about time you were able to look out of them.
- o Mirrors - They are always so much nicer to look at when they sparkle.
- o Your car - It doesn't need to be in pieces for you to polish it.
- o Coins.

It doesn't even matter if you choose to polish something simply for the act of doing it. So you might not exactly need that jar of pennies to shine bright, but if counting them has distracted you for the first hour (see distraction number 43), why not let polishing them distract you for the next?

FREE

24 : I MADE THIS

As adults we are often snowed under a great weight of duty and responsibility. Even the best-managed roles can bring snippets of negative thoughts to us, and when depressed, these can be unbearable.

Personally, I think it is important to stay in touch with our childish nature; where appropriate, because it can often help us reveal that element of fun. Illnesses don't generally come with pleasant feelings, and in the case of depression; happiness is the greatest enemy.

The world of make-believe might be something we left behind with milk teeth and stabilisers, but now is the perfect opportunity to dig out your imagination and let it distract you.

Quick Tip

- Just for the sheer hell of it, try and make up your own language. You don't need to take exams or start writing letters in it, but perhaps the odd made-up word; or one taken out of context, will instigate a cheeky smile. Mike and I often say silly things to each other that no one else would understand, and these act as little reminders that it's great to have a giggle. So it might not be enough to drive depression out of our home altogether, but the point of distractions is that they all work together to drag you out of the gloomy woods.

- If you've already tried distraction numbers 6 or 49, perhaps you can combine what you've already done to create your own game. I recently made up a New Year's Eve quiz to entertain family, which combined various elements of other things we have played. It certainly helped me to enjoy a time of year that I have dreaded for many years previously, and that in itself is a great step forward.

- Perhaps you could make your own board game and utilise some of your other creative skills to complete it. (See distraction number 21.) Another idea is to think of some dares to challenge and entertain you and your friends. My sister used to dare my friend and I to eat tomato ketchup sandwiches, or run down the street with a sheet over our heads making ghost noises. It would have worked so well if the sheet didn't have the Mr Men all over it!

- Some computer games allow you to create your own levels and maps, and if you fancy a change from simply playing the game, why not see what you can create instead. This can be as time-consuming or involved as you want it to be, and is something that you can keep coming back to whenever it suits. It is up to you whether you choose to share your designs with other players, or simply keep them for yourself, but you shouldn't let this outcome dissuade you from giving this distraction a go.

Whatever you choose to do, don't let the depressed or grown-up you tell you that it is a waste of time. In my opinion, time having fun is always time well spent.

FREE

25 : COUNT THE SHEEP

Sleep and I are good friends: very good friends in fact. We, like all relationships, have had our disputes. Angry turns in bed accompanied by quiet huffs of frustration. Promises of long, peaceful nights together ruined by loud passers-by and intrusive streetlights. Despite the various problems, interruptions and bouts of insomnia, sleep and I still get along just fine.

In all seriousness though, sleep (in moderation) is an excellent soul-soother, and does not have to be confined to the twilight hours.

After the birth of her new baby, my sister learnt the true meaning of 'power napping', and found herself better understanding our father and his afternoon snoozes. Going for a lie down during the day became a luxury; not something we only did when feeling ill.

Having forty winks can be an excellent distraction, not only for the physical benefits, but because asides from the odd dream or two, your mind truly gets its chance to switch off and de-clutter.

There were many times during my struggle with self-harm when the anger, tears and frustration tired me out so much, that having a lie down came naturally. What I discovered when I woke up was that I was much better able to calmly look at my situation and make rational; not emotional decisions.

Allowing myself to sleep at key moments honestly helped me avoid those bad decisions (such as cutting myself or pushing my friends away), and this in turn helped me take tiny steps towards my recovery. Like all of the distractions in this book, sleep is not the miracle cure to everything; more the helping hand in getting you to the positive place that you want, and deserve to be.

This might all sound like simple advice, but it is these obvious distractions that we often overlook. There is a great element of truth in the textbook 'things will feel different in the morning', but as mentioned before, clichés are all formed for a reason.

Quick Tip

- Even if you feel wide-awake right now and are tangled in a problem or negative feeling, find a nice quiet spot and try to rest. Focus on your breathing and allow yourself to relax. You might choose to lie down in bed, on the sofa, or out in the garden. It's up to you. Wherever you feel comfortable, head there now and see if you are able to nap.

- You don't have to have a full nights sleep to be rested. Even if you can only spare an hour or two, it is still worth it.

- If it's the middle of the day and you find it hard to sleep while the sun is out, then draw the curtains or invest in a light-blocking eye-mask.

- Perhaps you are at work and it is inconvenient for you to disappear off for a lie down. If so, why not make a plan to have a kip in your lunch break. I've often had a sleep in my car at work when I've not been feeling too well, and it has worked wonders. Just remember to set an alarm on your phone to wake you up again.

FREE

26 : CUT IT OUT

I must admit to feeling slightly apprehensive about using the term 'cut it out' in a book that started life as manuscript to help self-harmers, but rest assured that this title actually refers to scrapbooking.

Now scrapbooking may not be something that you've ever imagined doing in your life, but it is a wonderful distraction because the idea changes meaning depending on who you talk to. You are free to define this distraction in any way you want, which makes it so much more personal and worthwhile.

Some may find that they want to keep a scrapbook full of photos and ticket stubs; others may collect magazine cuttings and stamps in theirs. The general idea of a scrapbook is to hold memories of a time, place or person, but it really is completely up to you.

Quick Tip

If you need a place to start, why not begin with one of the following suggestions: -

- Cut out any stories that inspire you or give you hope. Keep them together somewhere, and flick through them when you need a little reminder of the positives.

- Perhaps there are words of encouragement you have found in either this book or another. Copy them down in your scrapbook and read them again. The beauty is that you are free to choose whatever is personal to you, and this is always going to have the greatest impact. I often found one persons account of self-harm far more comforting than whole textbooks on depression, and my only regret is that I assumed I wouldn't forget the sentences I found most helpful. I guess I'll just have to read those books again!

- Cut out words and pictures from magazines and newspapers to create a montage of how you feel. This is far easier than trying to write about it; especially if you've never been good at describing your emotions. Your montage could also be useful to help other people understand - such as your friends, family or therapist. It will be great for you to look back on this when you need a reminder that your feelings have changed. During my recovery I always found it impossible to accept that I was getting any better, and it was only looking over some of the things I wrote in my worse times, that I finally accepted I was making progress.

- Why not keep a scrapbook of something specific that interests you. Mine would be a collection of facts and pictures about ancient Egypt, or maybe a box full of patterns and ideas for new and unusual sock creations. (See distraction number 4.) Anything that reminds you of stuff that you enjoy is worthy, as these are often the things that we forget about whilst battling mental illness.

One of the wonderful things about this idea is that whilst it is a distraction that fits into the here and now, it can also be carried with you into the future. Scrapbooking is something that you work on and add to all the time, and so never has a limit on how much it can be enjoyed.

Every now and again when I am tidying our home I come across little reminders as to the person I used to be. My hobbies and interests used to be very different, and it is always interesting to remind myself of those changes. My memories of those childhood years are often of a difficult and tormented time, yet little scraps of the positives show me that there are other aspects of myself I may have forgotten about.

Ultimately, scrapbooking can be a solid affirmation of the good, for you to use in this treacherous battle against the bad. It might be an unlikely weapon, but it tends to be those smaller, seemingly insignificant elements of our lives, which help us win the fight with depression.

FREE

27 : FIND A FORUM

One of the beauties of this modern, technological age is that whatever it is that you want to talk about; there probably already exists a forum on the subject.

If (like I used to be) you are addicted to self-harm, there are places online where you can seek help. Many of them have specific threads where you can post a message to ask for support needed straight away, and there is usually someone else in the world online at that very moment who might just be the one to say something that stops you cutting yourself tonight.

You might use a forum as somewhere where you can share your stories and know that other people might be in similar situations, and this can be a great way to feel more connected in the world. However, I have to recommend forums specifically focussed around mental health problems with a tiny pinch of salt. As much as they can be fantastic, I have also personally experienced how overwhelming they can be, and this has also hindered my own recover.

On the forum pages of an excellent self-harm website, I found myself becoming extremely attached to and distressed by the suffering displayed, and it upset me that I simply couldn't help enough. No matter how much wisdom and experience I tried to share, there would always be another person who I couldn't reach. I logged on feeling strong and in control, and logged off feeling desperately hopeless.

On a more positive note however, it is worth noting that not everyone is affected in the same way, and although this particular forum wasn't right for me, it could be exactly what you need. Don't let my experience put you off.

Instead, keep it in mind so that you can notice if you are beginning to find it difficult too.

As with any online communication, it is extremely important to enter into it knowing that things can be misread, to appreciate that there will always be someone who winds you up, and to recognise when it is time to back away. Please also take the time to read any forum rules before you start posting, as breaking those guidelines isn't going to make for the best entrance.

Quick Tip

- You don't have to distract yourself with a forum designed specifically for whatever it is you need distracting from. Why not join a forum about something you take pleasure in. I take great satisfaction from finding and sharing special offers, and so frequently read posts on a UK deals forum. At moments when I have felt urges to self-harm, I have instead made use of a discount voucher found on the site.

- There are some great forums online about different aspects of money, and most of us could learn something from many of the comments made. Why not see if you can save your pennies by switching accounts, or if anyone has advice about getting out of debt. There might be a useful post about how to save for that (fill in the blank), or a link to a deal which you didn't know existed.

- Think about your hobbies and try to find a forum relating to one or more of them. Are you a keen gardener? Perhaps you can share tips online, or find out once and for all what that pesky bug on your apple tree is. Or maybe you want to share fashion advice or get opinions on a new style. If you are counting down the days to a specific holiday, you could ask any questions you have about the destination on a travel forum.

Whilst these are just examples of some of the more obvious topics, you might be surprised by just how many of the more obscure forums are out there.

FREE

28 : LET OUT THE BRITISH IN YOU

If there is one cliché that is true about Great Britain, it's that we love a good cup of tea. A well-made cup of tea can be warming after a brisk winters walk, and will refresh you after a sweltering trek through a desert holiday. An offer of a cup of tea at just the right time can feel like a blessing, and each sip can soothe the soul.

Don't forget that a cup of tea is also more than just the enjoyment of drinking it. Making this hot drink acts a perfect break from whatever it is you are doing; and is possibly contributing to your current mood. Heading off to the kitchen might take you away from a situation that you are finding stressful, giving you a much-needed moment to recompose yourself.

Whenever I am angry, depressed, tired or fed-up, Mike makes me a lovely hot cup of Earl Grey. Sometimes the first step in combating depression is breaking its grip on your routine (or lack of) and it is these simplistic acts, which make an excellent starting point. Of course tea can't make miracles happen, but it often feels just right at the time, and hence it is worthy of being here amongst these distractions.

Quick Tip

- Remember that there are so many different varieties of tea you can try. If you're not so keen on one type, try another. Different brands of tea can also taste quite unique, so you might just want to switch to another manufacturer.

- If you are looking to cut back on caffeine; how about a decaffeinated or fruit tea? Or if tea really isn't your thing, sipping a cup of coffee, hot chocolate, hot fruit squash or boiled water can be just as soothing.

- Why not make a flask of tea next time you go out for a walk, or are distracting yourself with some other activity? I've often paused on a day out to find a nice quiet seat where I can pour myself a cuppa. You wouldn't believe how many jealous looks we get from passers by!

FREE (IF YOU HAVE A CAMERA)
TO

29 : SNAP IT

No, not the neck of that annoying colleague up on fifth! Or even that pencil collecting dust on your desk. I use the verb 'snapping' here to mean taking photos.

I know many people who would happily go on holiday without a second thought for a camera, and I still can't quite believe it. One of the first things I do before I even begin to pack my suitcase is to check that mine is charged and that the memory card is suitable empty. Taking photographs has become second nature to me; even though it's not something I have ever studied or dedicated much time to. Although I rarely venture away from the fully automatic mode, simply using the camera to point and shoot is enough for me.

But taking photographs doesn't have to only be something you try whilst trekking through the jungle or rubbing noses with a lion. Photography can be an excellent distraction; whether you simply follow your pet around the house trying to capture that moment when he gives a great yawn, or lie down in the garden to discover the best way to take a photo of a single blade of grass.

Anything can be photographed, and at any time of day or night. This is exactly what makes photography so wonderful.

Quick Tip

- If you've never owned a camera, see if you can source a cheap one to start with, or perhaps borrow one from a friend. It doesn't matter if it's not the best quality; you just need something to get you going. Don't let yourself get too caught up in the amount of megapixels. Part of taking a great photo is about the way you frame the shot; and this you can practice with any camera.

- If digital isn't your thing (I'm still not a massive fan) dig out that old film camera, charge up the batteries, and start snapping the things around you. Some of my best photos have been taken with a very old film camera; which still has a very endearing 'feel.' You might even decide to take this distraction to the next step and start to develop your own photographs.

- Don't be afraid to play with all the settings on your camera. Try out the various modes and see what difference they make. I've ended up with some lovely, unusual photos from trying out a 'colour swap' mode, and it's been great fun experimenting. Don't be afraid to look at the instruction manual so that you can better understand exactly what your camera is capable of.

- Another side to this distraction is to simply look at photos you already have. Perhaps there are some old pictures in your family that you've never seen, or maybe some classic shots of you as a baby? Are there photos that need restoring or reprinting? Or maybe you could gather some favourites for an album. My friend put together a wonderful photo book in memory of her beloved cat, and it served as a beautiful keepsake. My only word of caution here would be to not dwell on photographs that evoke more painful memories. Try and keep this distraction positive and move on if you notice that you are feeling worse.

FREE

30 : GET WASHING

When we are feeling as though life is more of a burden than a blessing, it is often the mundane things such as keeping our home tidy that suffer with us.

I used to find that even the simple act of washing my clothes was too much hassle; and this isn't just because I was a lazy teenager. It was simply that I could not find the strength of mind to co-ordinate the action, and in my depressed state, I could never find a valid answer when I asked myself 'what's the point?' In Hindsight, I've noticed that forcing myself to do even such seemingly boring things helped me to then muster the strength to cope with much bigger problems.

Most of us will to some extent take pride in the way we look, and naturally this ties-in very closely with what we choose to wear. Clothes are therefore more than just a necessity; yet keeping them clean can often fall by the wayside when depression has us captive.

It doesn't matter if you have enough clothes to last you almost a year without washing a single thing, no-one wants to live surrounded by a pile of festering socks. My problem is exactly that: I don't need to do my washing because there is always something else to wear. However, recently I have realised that in a curious way, it is very satisfying to gather up all those dirty clothes, scrunch them up into the ball of a washing drum, and then pull them out of the machine smelling fresh and cool an hour or so later.

Suddenly I started noticing that I did actually take pride in my appearance, and I began to enjoy getting dressed each day with the knowledge that what I wanted to wear would be clean. It also gave me a sense of achievement when I took time to fold away my clean clothes, making space on the drier for wet washing to hang. If the weather is on my side; which is a very rare occasion indeed, then taking the laundry out into the garden gives me a great excuse for fresh air; which most of us can admit to needing more of.

I appreciate it sounds ridiculously obvious and basic, but depression is a very repetitive cycle, and it is often the mundane things that help us break it. One small step at a time, if you will. Cleanliness doesn't have to be a chore or a burden. If you allow it the chance, washing can be an extremely cathartic distraction.

Quick Tip

- Ignore those negative thoughts telling you there is no point, and force yourself to tackle that pile of dirty pants. If you are lucky enough to have someone else usually take care of your laundry, give them a night off and take over the responsibility yourself.

- Make a point of checking the washing instructions on the labels of your clothes, and follow them accordingly; even if it means you will have to do multiple wash loads. I find that the more I appreciate simple things such as what temperature my favourite jumpers should be washed at, the more proud I feel for knowing that I'm taking care of them.

- If you don't understand the different settings on your machine, perhaps now is the time to ask someone, or look up the instructions on the Internet. If you don't have a washing machine at home, making a trip to the laundrette is an equally great distraction.

- Similar to doing laundry, washing-up dirty dishes is also a brilliant distraction, especially when we can physically see the difference we are making. Having our hands in warm water is particularly soothing, and scrubbing yesterday's stubborn cereal off its bowl can make for a great way to vent some anger or frustration. Just steer clear of those fragile items if your mood means that you might not be as careful with them as you should be.

FREE TO 🐷

31 : A QUARTER OF

There is something extremely satisfying about tucking into a white paper bag full of penny sweets. Whether you are a kid returning from the local shop, or an adult re-living your youth by discovering your favourites are available to order online; sweets can serve more purpose than just keeping your dentist in business.

After a particularly rubbish week, I returned home to a brown box in the post containing contents that would make most kids squeal in delight. Sugary cola cubes, squishy foam bananas, pink and white vampire teeth, and innocently un-fishy prawns lay in wait for me; begging to be picked out first.

Whilst my excitement may have only lasted as long as the time it took for my stomach to moan with nausea and my teeth to feel 'hairy', the joy of 'I remember those' stifled the disdain I felt towards my job long enough for me to enjoy the rest of my evening. Surrounded by sweets, I actually 'forgot' about feeling crap and 'allowed' myself the breathing space I needed.

Naturally I believe that everything should be in moderation, and so would not condone the idea of replacing healthy fruit and vegetables with their sugary counterparts. I do, however, believe that a nostalgic treat now and then could work wonders for your mental health.

Quick Tip

- Try and make a list of all the sweets you remember eating throughout your childhood, and see how many of them you can find now. Do they taste different to how you remember?

- Experiment with different flavour jelly beans. Can you combine flavours to make something new?

- Help someone smile by making them a mini tuck-shop hamper. Think about the year they were born, and try to find sweets that you think they might have grown up with. Whilst we might think everyone knows what a Wham bar is, our grandparents might not agree.

FREE

32 : A VIDEO FOR EVERYTHING

If you think about how ridiculously complex using the Internet as a distraction can be (see distraction number 12), the least I could do is give YouTube it's own chapter.

I have an extremely inquisitive nature, and I'm sure that there are times when we all feel the urge to indulge our curiosity. YouTube is fantastic for just that, and offers the possibility of wasting extremely large portions of time.

Mike and I spent a rather large chunk of one weekend playing eighties cartoon intro's to see if the other one could remember which show it came from. (We reminisced so much that we later moved onto ordering that rather substantial box of old fashioned penny sweets from an online sweet shop.) The point is, on a day when we would otherwise have allowed the drizzly grey day to bore and depress us; we found our own simple distraction and made it into an entertaining time-consumer. As I tend to be the sort of person who quickly finds myself feeling negative if left without something to focus on, YouTube becomes the perfect distractor.

The great thing about this is that it doesn't matter when you need a distraction. It can be all kinds of unsociable hours, and YouTube will still be there. You can even download a podcast, which will store a selection of top videos on your mobile device ready for watching offline; if you are worried about not having an Internet connection.

I know all too well how heavy depression feels, and how even the most simple of tasks will evolve into a serious hurdle. There have been days when everything feels pointless, yet doing absolutely nothing still allowed the misery to spread within me. If my decade with depression has taught me anything, it is that doing nothing doesn't work. Watching short, often pointless videos on YouTube is the perfect distraction because it requires very minimal commitment in terms of energy, concentration or time, and yet thanks to the millions of people who upload to their servers, YouTube has so much to give.

Quick Tip

- If you have nothing in particular that you want to search for on YouTube, why not see if any videos out there can make you laugh. Look for jokes, cartoons or blunders - there are videos out there to suit all tastes.

- Don't forget that YouTube can also act as the distraction to help all other distractions. If you are trying to learn something like a language, or a how to cook that recipe you always wanted to try; there is more than likely a video out there which might give you some tips.

- If you have decided to plan a day out or holiday, perhaps someone has uploaded footage of the location you are interested in? This might help with the choices you are making, especially if the place is new to you.

- The possibilities of YouTube are endless and ever changing; so do use it to help you with other ideas in this book.

FREE

33 : ALPHABETISE

Organising is one of those things that many of us dread doing, yet it is actually strangely satisfying once we really get going. The difficulty is always in starting.

Our house is notoriously messy - so much so that I swear some people try to avoid visiting, but somehow in my darker moments I find the thought of tidying too much to deal with. I've always had piles of books, DVDs and CDs lying around, and if they do ever find themselves onto my shelves; they are often in no particular order.

I can't recall exactly what made me decide to one day alphabetise my collections, but I do remember that it was during an evening whilst I was fighting a fairly difficult bout of depressive thoughts. Somehow I was drawn to this distraction because it needed no creative input or serious brainpower, yet it was involved enough to force me to give it some concentration.

Perhaps this is just personal to me and you may read this and think 'no thanks,' before turning the page quickly, but I actually found myself enjoying this distraction. It certainly made finding my things much easier, and even though they quickly unsorted themselves again, I felt I'd exerted a little bit of control in my life.

Quick Tip

- Clear yourself some space on that bookshelf and replace your books or DVDs back in alphabetical order. Don't worry if you have to keep moving them back and forth - it's all part of the fun. The same can be done with your CDs too. (I have to admit I've never given this one a go myself - mostly because I tend to keep my music in collections of what I listen to the most.)

- This might also be a good opportunity to write a list of your collections so that you can better keep track of what you have. I started to do this with my DVDs, partially so that I could see exactly how much money I was spending on them, but also so that I could make a note of who had what when I began lending them to friends. I'm not suggesting that you go so far as to create your own lending library membership cards for your younger sister, but you have to admit it is nice to keep track of the things we've spent hard-earned money on.

FREE

34 : SING-A-LONG

Some of us do it in the shower; others prefer the privacy inside the bubble of a car. It doesn't matter if you are tone-deaf, note-perfect, or so shy that you can barely whisper a song; singing is something that all of us should try.

Music can be a great form of therapy, and this distraction naturally falls into the same category. When you are singing to your favourite tunes, often time passes without you even having to work at it. The sounds that come out of your mouth might even surprise you, and focusing on getting each lyric right offers a great excuse for your mind to concentrate. You might even find that the sound of your own voice helps to soothe you; or perhaps your loved one will appreciate your performance.

It doesn't matter what ability you are, or think you are at; learning to sing is still something that anyone can try. However, if you start to belt out that first note and your pet cat scurries out of the room with its ears folded; this might be a good indication that you still have a lot of practice to do. Don't be put off though - practice makes a great distraction.

Quick Tip

- Make yourself a playlist of your favourite songs (perhaps the same one from distraction number 9) and see if you can sing-a-long to the tracks. This isn't about preparing yourself to enter the 'X-Factor', so don't worry about reaching a professional standard. You can mumble the songs quietly to yourself, or scream them out to your heart's content. Do whatever you feel comfortable with (but try not to disturb any sleeping families). Remember that your range might not be the same as the artist, so you may need to change the key.

- For a different day out, take a look to see if any cinemas in the area have sing-a-long film nights. They often show classics such as 'Wizard of Oz' or 'The Rocky Horror Picture Show' and have subtitles running along the bottom so that the audience can join in with the songs. The idea might be terrifying or make you spontaneously cringe, but remember that when everyone gets into the spirit of it, inhibitions can be left at the ticket booth in trade for a fun few hours.

- If you'd like to take this distraction a bit more seriously, perhaps it is worth looking at getting some singing lessons. There are plenty of books to choose from if you'd like to teach yourself; otherwise it might suit you better to find a tutor. This will naturally involve learning to breathe and stand correctly; all of which can benefit you outside of singing.

FREE

35 : CHECKMATE

A good game of chess can be a great way to focus your mind on something other than misery, and all this great technology we have nowadays means that you won't even need another person to play against.

Chess is challenging and forces us to use our brains; which has got to be a good thing. It's also a game that has a definitive goal and end point, which makes it a far more desirable distraction than something which could continue forever. This might sound surprising, but if you think about the fact that depression feels so endless, it is often easier to fill your time with smaller, manageable goals, than it is to embark on a task where the ending is nowhere to be seen - This can feel overwhelming, and is more likely to strengthen those negative feelings if we fail to succeed.

Winning a game of chess can provoke a tiny boost in our self-confidence, and even losing doesn't feel so bad if the game has been challenging overall. My dad has always been excellent at the game and I used to play him a lot. If I was just able to keep my King safe for a few turns, then I would always feel as though I had accomplished something; even when he inevitably won.

Quick Tip

- Dust off your old chess set and see if you can find someone who would be interested in joining you for a game. If you or they have never played before, then now is the time to start. Don't worry about how long the game takes or who wins - this isn't about training to be a pro.

- Although I much prefer to play chess with a real board in front of me, virtual chess does serve a purpose. Playing against the computer is especially useful if you need a distraction at unsociable hours, or even if you simply don't feel like seeing anyone at the moment. The great thing about playing on the computer is that you can set your difficulty level at the beginning (- don't make the game too challenging, but don't make it too easy either.) If you don't have a chess game on your computer or console, simply do a search online for a free one. (There is a chess application on FaceBook that you could try, or perhaps you could download one of the ones available on iTunes to use on your device.)

- If neither of those quick tips appeal to you, why not simply do a search to find the variety of chess sets out there. My first ever pay cheque was spent on an Alice in Wonderland chess set, even though I really can't explain what made me so eager to buy it. Some of them can be beautiful to look at; even if completely impractical to play, and it can be quite fun to hunt for your favourite. I recently bought a Lego knights and skeletons chess set on our last visit to Legoland. It's great fun to look at and play with; especially when you can animate the moves to bring the pieces to life.

FREE TO

36 : GET PAMPERING

I am a firm believer that you can never pamper yourself too much. On a shallow level, yes - the more you do it, the less you perhaps need it, but taking care of our appearance and sense of wellbeing is one of those distractions that gives us something to concentrate on. Pampering happens to pass the time without us often noticing, and also gives us a confidence boost to help us retaliate against those negative thoughts.

I can honestly say that there have been occasions when my self-esteem has been at its very lowest, and I've distracted myself by deciding to spend an evening pampering. I might have been all dressed up with nowhere to go, but by putting on some make-up (ironic because I never wear it) and digging out some nice clothes; I've gone to bed that evening feeling a little better about myself. This can also be a way to discover a new style, if you do perhaps fancy a change.

Quick Tip

- As much as it might seem unnatural to you right now, try and find a way to show yourself some TLC. Ignore those doubts whispering 'but what's the point, no one is going to see?' - Doing this for you alone is reason enough.

- Here are some pampering suggestions: -

    o Try out some make-up, and see if you can find a 'look' that suits you.

- o Style your hair; perhaps testing out some different hair care products.
- o Make the effort to dress up in nice clothes - perhaps it is time to give your wardrobe a makeover?
- o Trim your nails, then paint or polish them.
- o Take care of your feet. (See distraction 53.) Soak or massage those toes, then treat them to some luxurious foot lotion.
- o Apply a face-mask, then sit back and relax until it is time to wash it off.
- o Give your body an all over skin scrub to gently remove dead skin, or simply massage in some nice lotion to sooth any dry patches. (I tend to find that the former works nicely in the summer, whilst the later is better suited to the winter months.)
- o Take a nice relaxing soak in the bathtub. (See distraction number 47.)
- o Give yourself a careful shave, then relish in how smooth your skin feels afterwards. (See distraction number 54.)
- o Try and make your environment nicer. Perhaps some fresh flowers will brighten up you home, or some candles will help you to relax. I always find that an oil burner with some calming scented oils help to soothe away my stress.
- o Deliberately plan a day, or even just a few hours where you can focus on 'me time'. You could even book yourself in for a professional massage, facial, or other body treatment - it might be an expensive luxury, but we all need spoiling every now and again.

Stress-reducing activities such as these can be good for your health, so try and remember this on those occasions when you still feel that you need an excuse to pamper yourself.

It is also important to remember that in order to help our loved ones, we need to take care of ourselves first. Pamper yourself for the simple reason that it will prepare you for when others need your help. I spent many years naively thinking that I didn't matter as long as I was good to others, but I had misunderstood the exact role that I played in this. What help could I be to anyone if I was total mess myself? One could even argue that you should pamper yourself *because* you care so much about other people.

FREE TO

37 : CLEAN THE CAR

Often when we are feeling downtrodden, it helps if there is something in our lives that we can take pride in. For many people, automobiles are exactly that. They do not just have to be a method for us to get from A to B. Cars can also be something that we cherish and take care of. Part of this naturally involves keeping them clean and tidy.

As with many things, when you can step back and instantly see the difference you have made, it is hard not to feel even just a tiny bit of satisfaction. Personally, I find driving much more enjoyable after I have made the effort to tidy up my car, and driving in itself can also be another distraction. (See distraction number 44.)

Cleaning in its own right can be cathartic, but scrubbing the dirt off your car has an added bonus - it involves getting you outside for fresh air, and if you are lucky enough; some sunshine. (See distraction number 8.)

Quick Tip

- It doesn't matter what time of day it is, grab a bucket and sponge (or a hose if they aren't banned in your area) and get to work cleaning the outside of your car. If you don't own one, I'm sure your family, friends, or neighbours would happily let you clean their cars instead - but make sure you ask them first.

- Once the outside is clean (or if you would prefer to start here,) get to work on the interior. Throw away all those old parking tickets and empty water bottles, and give your mats and seats a good vacuum. If you really want to go to town on it, then get hold of some special dashboard cleaner and window wipes, and give them a good scrub also.

- If you really can't stand the thought of manually washing your car, then perhaps it is time you drove it down to the local car wash. Petrol stations often have automatic ones, but do remember that there are also places where you can get your car hand-washed for the same price - or possibly even less than a garage will charge. In our household we often get our cars hand-washed in the car park of our local supermarket while we pick up our weekly shop. Whilst this still does get you out of the house, for this distraction to really work best, I would recommend that you wash your car yourself.

FREE

38 : WHERE IS THAT MISSING PIECE?

I have to admit that this is one of those curious distractions that does seem so glaringly obvious and sensible when I think about it, yet it is one that I rarely got around to doing.

Jigsaw puzzles can distract our minds wonderfully by engaging us in a challenge, and then rewards us with a firm sense of achievement when completed. I've often been amazed at how time appears to scurry past me whilst I slot crooked pieces of card together, and this is all time spent away from the noose of depression and my self-harm crutch.

Quick Tip

- Dig out that jigsaw, create a nice clean space to start it, and give the puzzle a go. Don't concern yourself over details such as how long it will take; you can come back to it as and when you need to. It might therefore be wise to make a start on a table that you don't need to use in the immediate future, as it'd be frustrating if you have to break up the puzzle so you can eat dinner. Maybe there is a quiet spot on the floor you could use instead? Eventually you might find that it is worthwhile investing in a puzzle board, so that you can fold up your work and move it aside without disturbing the completed parts.

- If you don't already own a jigsaw, see if you can buy a cheap one. Some second-hand shops sell jigsaw boxes that have never been opened, or there are shops and places online that you can choose from. I wouldn't recommend getting the largest and most difficult one you can find; else it might put you off even starting it. Begin small and with a fairly easy jigsaw, then if you find yourself enjoying this distraction you can always work your way up.

- See if you can find a strategy that works for you. Some people like to sort the pieces into edges and middle sections; others divide by colour. Or maybe you prefer to work by locating specific pieces according to the picture on the box? Give all of the above methods a go and see which you prefer.

- One less obvious variation of this distraction is to actually make your own jigsaw. You could either draw or paint something onto some sturdy card, or print out a picture or photograph, which can then be glued onto card. Carefully divide the whole piece into sections, and then cut out your jigsaw pieces. They can fit together any way you want, so don't worry if the pieces don't interlock.

Despite what the title of this chapter suggests, I would urge you to only attempt a jigsaw when you know all of the pieces are actually in the box. Stay clear of any that look suspiciously incomplete. There can be nothing more frustrating than not being able to finish the puzzle because the dog swallowed that bit right in the middle.

FREE

39 : MAKE YOUR OWN

Whilst cooking as a distraction already forms its own chapter (see distraction number 2), there are other things that you can make in the kitchen, which I feel deserve a chapter of their own.

On a hot summer's day there is something very rewarding about making your own ice cream, especially if you are partial to some of the more unusual flavours out there. (Cardamom is one of my favourites, but I'll be dammed if I can find anyone who still sells this.)

Smoothies, milkshake, punch and yoghurt are also very simple to make, and require much less effort in the kitchen than a roast dinner with all the trimmings. You also don't need to use the oven to make them, and if your oven is as temperamental as ours; then not using it has got to be a bonus.

I am a firm believer that our society of convenience has many questions to answer about the lack of satisfaction that we often experience in our lives. It might be easier to simply go to the supermarket and buy a ready-made smoothie, milkshake or whatever, but this isn't going to help us establish a sense of self-worth. This isn't a life-changing feeling on its own, but tiny bouts of fulfilment make up part of the weapons that we use to keep depression at bay.

Quick Tip

- Next time you feel yourself getting stressed, direct your energy towards making one of these: -

- o Smoothie
- o Milkshake
- o Ice cream
- o Yoghurt
- o Fruit Punch

- Don't be afraid to experiment with ingredients - the worst that can happen is that you have to tip it down the sink and start again. On the upside, you might discover a wonderful combination of flavours that you simply can't buy in the shops.

- I might have used the example 'on a hot summer's day,' but this distraction can, and should be used whatever the weather. Who says you can't eat freshly made ice cream while it happily snows outside? I know I do!

- If you find that you really start to enjoy making your own, perhaps you can invest in a machine or two to help you along the way. Our ice cream maker might be a tad noisy, but it certainly beats stirring our creation every hour to break up the ice crystals.

FREE

40 : BACK-UP

This might sound like a curious distraction, but as anyone working with computers will tell you; it is extremely important. It's not the most interesting of ideas, but if you somehow find a way to discard everything else in this book, it's time to back-up the data on your computer.

Working in I.T. and dealing with lost data on a weekly basis, I know how easy it can be to lose valuable files; yet most of us never bother to back-up. In fact, it's usually those of us who work with computers the most that take them for granted - but we would also be the ones tearing our hair out if they died.

A few years ago I came home from dinner, put my laptop on the living room table and sat down on the sofa with my best friend and a cup of tea to chat the night away. We must have been there for almost an hour before we decided to go and play on the Xbox upstairs. Unbeknown to us, someone had broken in before we got home and was hiding in my housemate's room for that full hour; waiting for us to leave so they could escape through the front door - with my laptop and handbag. I was terrible at keeping up-to-date back-ups, and needless to say, I lost a lot that night.

Nowadays I back-up much more frequently, and find that there is something strangely satisfying about making a copy of those important files on an external hard drive or DVD. After all, the last thing you need when you are already feeling so negative is to find out that you've lost your life's writing, or holiday memories.

Something like a back-up can be great at taking your mind off things because it forces you to focus. As you browse all the files on your computer you might also find that you are distracted with data that you forgot you even had. Perhaps you will stumble over an old photo or a favourite song that brings a smile to your face? Whilst one photo isn't going to be a miracle cure to depression, it can be that tiny reminder of something positive; in a moment that feels so grey and wretched.

Quick Tip

- Remember that some data can be kept in not-so-obvious places, and so are easy to miss. If you are running Windows, make sure you back-up anything on your desktop, and settings or files that specific software might store in their own directories. In OS X, you might want to back-up your preference (plist) files, and other data in the Library directory. Whichever operating system you use, it's not just documents that need backing up; don't forget about your contacts, Internet favourites, mail archives, music and photos.

- There are existing methods whereby data can be backed up automatically, but it is still worth doing a manual one yourself. Sometimes the automatic process can skip files that might be duplicated, or might even fail altogether due to an error in communication. Not to mention that when you first set up the back-up, you might have accidently excluded directories which actually you now need to include. It won't hurt to make another copy; and remember to store this somewhere separate from your main data. There is no point having a back-up which could just as easily get lost.

- If your computer is fully backed-up, can you say the same about your mobile phone or handheld device? Make sure you have all the contacts and photos from these stored elsewhere. You never know when your phone, iPad or similar could break or get lost.

FREE

41 : FIND THE WORDS

Something my cognitive behavioural therapist once taught me to try was to write a letter to a person who has hurt me, without the intention of ever giving it to them. The idea was to get me thinking about what I would say in a totally honest, yet secure way. Knowing that this person would never read the letter helped me to focus on how I truly felt, and this in turn helped me to move forwards with my recovery.

Surprisingly, I learnt from my writing that I actually felt angry towards a certain person for the things they put me through, yet up until that point I only ever knew that I felt fear. This discovery opened new doors for me, but they were ones that ultimately helped me to find closure.

Quick Tip

- Write a letter to someone you feel angry towards, hurt by, or scared of. Explain how your emotions have developed, and tell them the part they played. Think about what you would want to say to them if you had the chance or strength. Remember this isn't a letter that you need to send. It's the actual act of writing it that counts here.

- How about keeping a diary of how you feel; making note of how your mood changes at different times of the day? Do you notice a pattern? This might help you to plan things to occupy your mind during your low points, which could help uplift, and keep your mood more stable. Being aware of a pattern might also help you to 'go easy' on yourself at times when you feel hopeless, because you can be reminded that these emotions do always shift; even if only slowly or very slightly.

- If you don't feel ready to face these often strong and crippling emotions, why not write a letter to a stranger; such as a pen pal? As mentioned in distraction 46, I've started writing letters to a prisoner in Bangkok, and this has been very cathartic for me - as well as interesting for the recipient. There are a few prisoner support charities who can offer advice to get you started, and you can of course choose who you'd like to write to. I also find that reading my letters from Thailand help me to put my own life in better perspective, as it reminds me of the things I take for granted. This is a positive reaction, despite the fact that comparisons often make me feel more negative.

FREE

42 : CAPTURE THE FLAG

Computer games are such an excellent distraction, that millions of people in the world pretty much live to play them. We've all met them; you know, that quiet one at work who spends their weekends slaying dragons, and talks about it on Monday morning as if it is 'real' life. My fiancé was one of them! I'm not saying you should become that obsessed with virtual reality, but everyone should have a bit of game-playing in their lives.

Playing games combines some of the best elements of other distractions: they force you to concentrate on specific goals, reward you for your hard work, and leave you feeling satisfied and often worn out. When you are immersed in a game, you are allowed to forget about yourself, your life - and the problems with both, and become whoever you want to be. You can't of course spend all your time wishing that you really were a shoe-wearing blue hedgehog, but for that moment you are playing; you have no responsibilities, pressures, or commitments. This can be extremely refreshing, and that break from reality will often help you to feel strong enough to return to it.

With consoles such as the Wii making you actually leap up and work for that gold coin, you can even get a bit of exercise with this distraction, and we already know that not many people can claim to be getting too much of that.

I am lucky enough to have a great choice of games and consoles available to me because when Mike and I moved in together, our combined technology meant we had a Playstation, PSP, Xbox, Wii and Nintendo DS. In some cases, we even had one of every version (- we were definitely meant to be together). Often when I'm feeling fed up or sense that my mood is slipping, I will fire up the Wii and tire myself out sword fighting.

Quick Tip

- There are such a wide variety of games available on so many different platforms, that there is bound to be something that takes your fancy. If a game isn't available for your console; perhaps it is available for your PC or Mac computer, or vice versa?

- Have a think about the type of game you prefer to play, and explore ones that fit into that category. I prefer playing ones that don't hook you into a long and complex story because I hate the idea of committing to a game for long periods of time. Most of my collection is of mini-games, which you can start and finish in short spaces of time. I also love racing games that finish quickly, whereas Mike loves role-playing, adventure games, which he will continue for weeks. If you've never enjoyed computer games, have you ever thought that perhaps it is because you've not found the right type of game yet?

- If you're bored of the games you already have, maybe now it's time to treat yourself to a new one. If you want to make sure a game is worth the money before you buy it, have a look at the reviews available. Remember that you can often get them pre-owned for a cheaper price.

- Don't forget that there are also plenty of online games to choose from, or your computer may have even come with some built into the operating system. They might not be the most exciting games out there, but they will distract you just the same.

FREE

43 : COUNT THE COINS

This is one of those weird distractions that you rarely do, but is unusually satisfying!

I started putting coins away when I was a child colleting the Natwest piggybanks. (I only ever got the first three of them before they changed the scheme and gave out wildlife coins instead - my fourth pig came with Lady Hilary's head smashed off, which might have scarred me for life!)

I later got into the habit of emptying my wallet of all one penny, two pence, and five pence pieces, to fill up the pigs with and make my bag lighter. I never seem to spend them anyway, and would otherwise end up with such a large collection in my purse that it no longer zips up. The one thing I never really did however, was sort the coins out and pay them into my bank.

If you are anything like me and have piggybanks, old glass bottles, or a drawer full of coppers, now is the time to get some bank bags and count out the loose change in preparation for paying them into your account.

It might sound a bit desperate if you look at it as a way to use that extra bit of money (unless you have a massive piggybank full of hundreds of pounds!) but the key is to see the actual act of counting coins purely as a distraction, and to do it regardless of how much you end up with. It can be really satisfying to see the coins pile up into an amount that seems more usable, plus it is a great way to focus on something that needs a bit of concentration.

Quick Tip

- Put on some slouchy, comfortable clothes, sit yourself down with a nice beverage, and tip out those coins ready for counting.

- Automatic machines to count coins do exist, but where is the fun in that?! Although the end result will be the same, remember that this distraction is all about the count, so don't be tempted to go for the quicker option.

- Why don't you open a savings account especially for something specific? You can pay the coins into there. It might not seem like much, but you'd be surprised how all those pennies eventually add up, and every payment into that savings account is a step closer to your goal.

- If you're not already squirreling coins away, perhaps you can set aside a container to start collecting in from now on - if only so that you can use this distraction at a later date.

FREE

44 : DRIVE AWAY

Courtesy of my dad, I have a somewhat boyish interest in cars and I enjoy experiencing their subtleties. They are so much more than just a way to get around, and driving can be one of the most pleasurable things we can do on wheels.

Whilst I find myself using driving as a distraction from minor mood changes these days, at my most depressed of times getting in my car would have been a very bad move. If I were completely honest with myself, the intense anger I felt right before I used to cut myself would likely have caused me to crash my car if I had instead chosen to get behind the wheel. Not necessarily by accident either.

Everyone is different however, and going for a drive in your time of need might be the perfect distraction for you, without resulting in a hefty insurance claim.

Being in our cars can be such a great freedom because we can literally get lost in our little bubble. Driving can be time to be alone, or a chance to share the road with people we care about. We can play our music loud and sing to our hearts content; forgetting that no car is soundproof and people outside can actually hear us. I know that when I get in my car I feel in control (well you would hope so wouldn't you!) I feel alive, aware and free. The concentration that driving takes can also be a great way to expel unwanted energy, and this in turn can help us sleep and feel better for the morning. Just make sure that you stop the car before you even start to get tired.

Quick Tip

- If you don't drive, ask if someone else would be able to take you out. One of your friends might jump at the opportunity to take their car for a spin, or you might find that they too could use the distraction.

- Perhaps you could combine this with another idea from this book? Why not drive to somewhere you can go for a walk, or a place you can visit such as museum or shop. Maybe it is about time you went to visit friends and family?

- Personally I find that the music I play in my car can greatly influence the type of driver I am at that particular moment, and so I would urge you to choose something that will help you feel strong and independent; not something that is going to make you feel worse. (See distraction number 9)

Caution

Don't drive right now if deep down you know you'll be reckless. (If you slam that car door so loud that your neighbour's car alarm goes off, it's probably a good indication that you should get out the car, go back inside and try another distraction.)

FREE

45 : FIND A SPACE AND WATCH THEM

People can be extremely fascinating if we simply take the time to sit quietly and watch them. This has got to be one of my most used distractions, purely because it is easy, free and fantastic at passing time whilst waiting for something; usually a friend who is late to a meeting.

The second great thing about people-watching is that it is totally unpredictable and ever changing. Sometimes strangers will pass you by; quietly unaware you are admiring their dress-sense or hairstyle. Others will look or act so unusually that you can't help but give a little internal smile. This distraction is so brilliant because it can be a whole range of things: interesting, funny, scary or puzzling come to mind; there are too many to list. It is this view to expect the unexpected, which makes life so interesting, and can help us to break away from our personal soul-destroyers.

I love quietly watching the world go by because it also gives me an opportunity to see things that I wouldn't normally notice or appreciate. Sometimes I see places that I never knew existed, and other times it is the people who fascinate me. Waiting in a queue for a rollercoaster at Thorpe Park, whilst people-watching I saw a woman who was talking to a row of tiny dolls tucked into her bum-bag. I believe she was reassuring them that the ride wouldn't be too scary! Of course it would have been rude to stare or giggle at her slightly nutty ways, but noticing her took my mind off the wait, gave me a little story to tell later on, and also made me realise that my flirt with madness didn't mean I was too far gone - without meaning to sound nasty, this girl was far more bonkers than I'd ever been.

It is only human nature to make comparisons, but on this occasion a stranger helped me put my life in context. These little everyday realisations can make a surprising difference along the road to recovery.

Quick Tip

- Find a nice quiet spot to sit or stand, and watch the world go by. Allow yourself to explore how the people passing by make you feel.

- If you find it easier to focus on something specific for each person, ponder over one, some, or all of the following: -

  o   Fashion sense
  o   Hairstyle
  o   Type of walk
  o   Does the person look strong or weak?
  o   Where do you think they are going?
  o   What job do you think they do?
  o   Rich or poor?
  o   Guess how old they are

- Make sure you do keep these thoughts to yourself however; you don't want to accidently start insulting strangers - Remember this isn't about picking faults with others; it's just a way of distracting yourself from those negative elements in your life by observing the intricacies of human behaviour.

- If you are lucky enough (in my opinion) to be alone in your surroundings, stop and admire the landscape or places around you. Is there a shop, museum, or tourist location, which you'd never noticed before? Perhaps you might decide to come back and visit another day. Even if you are somewhere you have been to many times, chances are there will still be things you haven't seen.

FREE

46 : SHARPEN THAT PENCIL AND WRITE

How could I possibly write a book about distractions, and not put the actual act of writing as one of them! This distraction is one of my personal favourites, and you could say this very book was spawn of it. I literally wrote my way through depression and often forced myself to pick up a pen instead of a blade to cut myself with (I don't mean I cut myself with a pen!)

The great thing about writing is that there are no rules. It's not one of those things that once you've started you have to commit to it, and if you stop half way through writing something, you can go back to it whenever you want; or never at all.

Personally, I found writing about how I felt to be one of the key factors in my recovery. You would think one would get bored of writing about depression, but no! I wrote a whole book about it. Every time I put pen to paper a new way of explaining those feelings came out.

There are two main benefits to this. First is that you can use your writing to help other people try and understand what you are going through. Often it is impossible to find the words to talk to someone, yet try and write about it and suddenly the words are flowing.

Second, when I looked back over some of the chapters I wrote, it really did help me to understand depression better. To use a quote from myself, 'depression hates to be understood. When you begin to decipher it, it cannot spiral out of control, or attack you without warning.' Even if it is not depression that you are trying to fight, you will more than likely find that the

115

better you understand why this affects you, the easier it is to see a way to escape its clutch.

Of course I am completely bias because writing is something that feels quite natural to me, but it really is a skill that can be learned by anyone. Give it a go, and don't set yourself any targets to start with. Just write without purpose and see if it works for you. I wrote a third of my book without evening deciding I was writing a book - this is just as well because if I did have that goal in mind earlier on, I would never have started.

Quick Tip

- You don't have to write about how you feel if this is just going to trigger the negative emotions. Writing can be a distraction whatever you write about. How about your favourite memory, a funny moment in your life, or perhaps a work of fiction?

- Here are some other suggestions: -

  o Poetry can be an excellent place to start, especially if you've never really written much in the past. Remember, poems don't always have to rhyme.

  o If you think it might help, try and describe how you feel, and why you think this might be. Explain what self-harm means to you, and how it makes you feel like you are coping. Try and imagine that you are writing for someone who has never heard of anyone with your struggles before. What would you say to them?

  o How about writing a letter to a loved one, or perhaps to your friend or counsellor. (See distraction number 41.) Is there something you've needed to say? You don't even haven to give them the letter; just writing it can bring a great relief. If you'd rather write to a stranger, perhaps you can find yourself a pen-pal? I recently started writing to a Malaysian prisoner on death row in Thailand because it saddened me to know that he was away from his home country; sentenced for a non-heinous crime.

  o They say every person has a book inside them - try and get it out.

  o Have you ever written a diary? Now is the perfect time to start.

  o Grab a pad of paper and write down everything that flows

through your mind. It doesn't have to make sense and you don't even have to write sentences. Just put words down. This process can be called thought-streaming, and is great if you are feeling particularly angry or frustrated. I seem to remember writing quite a few pages of just 'fuck you' in my time.

o   It might sound silly, but why not write a shopping list? It will save you spending money on junk food and ingredients you already have, but coming home with nothing that you actually need.

Whatever you write, remember that the point of it is not for your words to be perfect. It doesn't have to be grammatically correct or spelt right. No one is judging your work.

Caution

If you've written a page that could take some explaining (I'm thinking 'I hate my boss' or 'I've always wanted to tell you that your hair looks crap') then be careful where you leave it. You don't need someone else's upset or anger cramping your recovery style.

Sophia Gill

47 : GET SOAKED

At some time in our lives, most of us will enjoy a soothing hot bath filled to the brim with bubbles. (Some of us just might not admit it!) Whether I'm feeling ill, cold, depressed or just bored; soaking in a quiet hot tub by the light of a candle or two always comforts me.

Perhaps it is the water that numbs the depression, or maybe the warmth subdues my negative thoughts. Whichever it is, taking a bath has always been a fantastic soul-soother, especially when I am feeling alone and fed up on a cold winter's night.

Let me just say however, that it doesn't matter what time of day or year it is. You can use this distraction whenever the time is right for you.

Quick Tip

- Let yourself feel indulged with your favourite bath bubbles and a cool glass of whichever refreshment you like. (I prefer plain water with ice cubes, as I tend to keep adding hot water to my bath until I overheat.) Light a candle, turn out the lights, and perhaps play some calming music in the distance (please remember that electricity and water don't mix - no stereos in the bathroom, OK!) Having a bath shouldn't just be about mundane cleaning; let it become something decadent and calming.

Whatever it is that makes taking a bath feel so nice, one thing is for certain: when our physical being feels good, so do our minds. Bathing also combines perfectly with distraction number 36 so don't be ashamed if you spend the next couple of hours pampering yourself.

FREE

48 : HEAR THE STORY

You might be surprised just how calming it is to get yourself comfortable and absorb yourself in an audio book. On many occasions I have tucked myself up in bed at 9pm; a warm drink by my side and a hot water bottle clutched to my tummy, just listening to the hypnotic voice playing from my stereo. It is almost like recreating the pleasure a child gets from having their parent read them a bedtime story; only without having to rely on another person to fulfil this need.

I tend to buy audio versions of books I have already read. This way, in the desperate, confused state of mind I am in when I have the urge to cut myself, listening to the book is made easier by the fact I already know the storyline. You may think this sounds boring; a bit like reading the same book twice, but for me, hearing the story spoken is like experiencing it for the first time. I also find myself drawn towards children's audio books, because their simplicity means I am more inclined to use them as a distraction. With less complicated, and often much shorter stories, I tend to find them less intimidating during those times when I need them most.

Quick Tip

- If you haven't already got an audio book lying around that you've been meaning to listen to, ask your friends and family if they have any which they can lend you. Otherwise, see if your local library rents them out. It doesn't even matter if its something you normally wouldn't pick up as a book; you might discover something new to enjoy.

- Why not browse the charity shops? You might find some old audio book cassettes for less than the cost of the equivalent C.D, or you might find a second-hand C.D. version for cheaper than you could buy it new.

- You don't have to stick to authors you know; why not browse online for reviews of books in genres you like.

FREE

49 : I KNOW THIS ONE

I've spent a lot of time trying to work out exactly how depression makes me feel, so that I can better understand and know how to fight it. One of my conclusions is that it makes you forget anything you think you know, and forces you to believe that you are this hollow, empty space without any sense of enjoyment.

Depression never banked on me figuring out how to conquer it, perhaps because the theory is so simple. One of the hardest steps is to constantly remind yourself that the feelings you have right now have not been, and will not be there forever - despite them making you believe that the opposite is true.

At my most depressed I felt as though I knew nothing, had no skills, and had zilch to offer the world. As well as using the other distractions in this book to remind you of the positive, fun things you have around you, it can also be useful to remind yourself of the knowledge you hold.

It sounds basic, and perhaps a little pointless, but have you ever thought about quizzes as a distraction?

Quick Tip

- Write a quiz about any topic you like and try it out on your friends and/or family. Many people really enjoy the challenge, and it can be a great confidence boost to see people having fun with it.

- If you can't get inspired to write one, try doing a quiz instead. There are plenty online, ranging from testing your knowledge of films or music, to analyzing your personality from the choices you make. Don't take the results too seriously however. It really doesn't matter if you don't get all the answers right, or the quiz tells you that your ideal job is snow ploughing.

The great thing about quizzes is that they subtly remind you about the things you *do* know - how many times do you curse yourself with 'I knew that one!' A quiz can also highlight the interests you have, and the enjoyment that you get from them. You might find yourself reminded about a great film you are dying to watch again, or even a hobby that you keep meaning to pick up.

When I saw and took a quiz about the TV show 'Dexter' after it was posted on my Facebook newsfeed, it made me remember how much I love this show. As simple as this sounds, it opened my eyes to the thought that I wasn't always feeling so terrible because at some point in time I was simply enjoying watching this great series. Of course I immediately dug out the box set and started watching it again, and so my enjoyment continued.

One distraction can easily lead to another, and you could argue that it is this stringing simple actions together, which life is all about.

FREE

50 : LOOK UP

Ever since I jumped out of a plane to raise money for charity, I found myself fascinated with everything above me. I would gaze longingly at the bright blue sky, thinking to myself 'it's a great day for a skydive'. Waiting at Waterloo station, I started looking around the vast building and found my eyes transfixed on the pigeons perched high up in the rafters, or on the lost helium balloon that clung to the roof; longing to break free. I began realising that there were intricate details on buildings that I had walked past many times before, but never even noticed.

Next time you are out and about, simply look up. You'll be amazed at what you have been missing.

Quick Tip

- Go outside and enjoy whatever is above you. Why not: -
    - o   Make shapes out of clouds.
    - o   Count the birds (or planes) that fly past.
    - o   Try and guess when a building was built from the architecture.
    - o   If it's raining outside, why not gaze up at the sky outside the window, and make yourself feel all snug and cosy for being indoors.

There are so many things to look at, and appreciating it all can have a very calming effect. It can also be quite amusing to notice how many people around you follow suit.

I was once looking up at lights around the Empire State building in New York one foggy evening. It was lit up with red, white and blue lights, and the red light shining through the fog almost looked like fire. Moments later, people on the street were also staring, and whispers quickly filled the street that the building was alight. A police car pulled up at the lights near me, and both officers got out of their cars to also stop and stare. They got on their radios immediately, and within minutes the lights had been turned off. Rather embarrassed about the commotion I had possibly started, I scurried away and made a mental note to be more subtle in future.

FREE

51 : OUT WITH THE OLD

If you are anything like me, there will be piles of 'stuff' around your house that you have never got around to sorting. Letters, magazines, and bills. Clothes that need washing, and clean clothes that need folding up and putting away. Whether you live alone, with family, or with your partner, it seems as though there is always something that needs to be done. Right now is the time to start.

Sifting through piles that you've been meaning to sort is a great distraction with an added bonus: you never know what you might find. There is also something quite cleansing about throwing away the things you don't need; and that is coming from someone who loves to collect!

It might be hard to find the energy to begin a task like this, so start small. Perhaps choose one pile of paperwork and tackle just that. Even if it just means sifting through it to make a new, smaller pile; it's a start. You might even find that once you get going, you start to enjoy it so much that you keep at it and don't even notice your spirits lifting.

Quick Tip

- Why not: -

    o Get rid of old clothes. Start with anything you know you don't wear and clothes that don't fit you anymore - be harsh, and don't hold onto things for 'sentimental value' I used to ask myself 'if I really did shrink two dress sizes, would I really want to wear this dress I've had for years, or would I probably want to buy a new one?' If clothes that don't fit you are making you depressed instead of giving you the incentive to get fit, then don't hang onto them.

o   Buy yourself a folder to keep important bills and documents together - and put them all in it. (Remember how frustrating it is when you need to buy your car tax and you can't find your insurance document or renewal letter.)

o   Clear the clutter from your desk (and don't just hide it in the drawers).

o Go through the kitchen cupboards and throw away those old jelly packets with best before dates that make you cringe - you're never going to eat them and your house isn't an antiques showroom. It might feel like a waste, but space isn't something most of us can sacrifice for spoiled food.

FREE TO

52 : PICK UP THAT BOOK, AND READ IT

I am probably quite bias about this distraction because books have always been extremely important to me. However, even if you class yourself as 'not much of a reader', you should still give this one a go. After all, if you have made it all the way through this book to get to idea number 52, you are already doing pretty well. Perhaps another book will captivate you just as much, if you only allowed yourself the chance to find it.

Books are, in my opinion, truly amazing. It is now possible to find a book about almost any subject, and the lists are growing every day. When I first started self-harming in the mid 90's, I struggled to find even one book that mentioned this taboo subject. Now I can pick one up from the supermarket with my pint of milk.

Reading can be one of the most powerful things that we can do, and I honestly believe that we can never do enough of it. Books allow us to learn without going to class, they enable us to understand difficult subjects from the safety of our sofas, and they can fill us with intrigue, hope, joy, fear and sadness, with the simple action of turning a page.

At my most depressed, I have to admit I did get rather obsessed with books, and lined them up on my shelf ready to be read. One of my fears was

129

finishing a book and not having another one to read, or wanting one that was a different style. In the end I bought myself paperbacks from all different genres, so that no matter what took my fancy next; there would be a book to suit. In short, I was desperate to ensure that I always had a distraction.

The large collection of books about mental illness that dominated my shelves were the ones I turned to most often, because the simple act of knowing I wasn't alone in my suffering was so very important to my state of mind. Sometimes there was advice in these books that I had never considered, and other times they opened my eyes to some of my own strengths and weaknesses. If there is a chance that you too can learn, or simply experience the comfort of feeling that someone out there understands, then this is a chance worth taking.

If you feel as though these emotional books might hinder your recovery, there are plenty of other subjects out there. A humorous book can be a great lift during difficult times, whilst a crime or mystery novel can involve you so much that you barely notice your own thoughts.

Quick Tip

- Glance at your bookshelf and see if there is a book or two that you've not read yet, or would like to read again. Perhaps someone in your family has something they can recommend, or a friend has a book they can lend you.

- If you're not sure what to pick, have a look at reviews online, or make a note of any that are recommended on television or in magazines.

- Have a think about what kind of genres to you like and perhaps start by looking at the top sellers in those categories. You will quickly learn which authors you like the best, and with any luck they will keep releasing new work.

- Don't forget that bookshops are not the only place you can buy books. Whilst I do think it is great to support your local bookseller, if you are on a budget, take a look in second hand shops. Otherwise, get yourself down to the local library.

- If you are a commuter or just don't like the idea of carrying a book around; digital books viewed on electronic readers can be a great solution. They allow you to carry more than one with you at any time, and if you can't 'get into' the first, you can always switch to something else.

Remember, if you never normally read much, don't start this distraction by picking the largest book you can find. You are much more likely to finish it if you start with something a bit smaller. I actually enjoy reading children's books when I'm feeling down, as they are much easier to read and often don't require as much time. Don't be embarrassed by whatever book you choose - it doesn't matter what other people think. I'm sure the first adult to read Harry Potter is sitting there thinking 'I told you it was good!'

Sophia Gill

FREE

53 : PUT YOUR FEET UP

At the beginning of one of my lunchtime Pilates classes that I attend at work, our instructor had us all sat on mats on the dusty floor of the drama hall, massaging our own feet. It felt like a strange start to the class, but later on I noticed that my feet felt awake. That evening; for want of something new to do, I announced to Mike that we were going to have a foot spa after dinner.

Balanced on the thin edge of our bath, we soaked our deserving feet in the hottest water we could cope with; scented with bath salts which I had forgotten we owned, and chatted about the nice food we wanted to cook that week. When our feet felt nicely warmed and tingly, we dried them off and applied generous amounts of cooling, minty foot lotion; massaging as we went.

Despite having spent the day feeling underappreciated, unenthusiastic, and unmotivated at work, I went to bed that evening feeling soothed and cared for. The simple act of resting and taking care of my feet had distracted me from the boredom of everyday life, and provided a nice break in our routine.

Quick Tip

• It doesn't matter if it's spring, summer, winter or autumn; soaking your feet in water will feel great. If it does happen to be so hot right now that the thought of the heat makes you feel dizzy, how about a refreshingly cool foot bath?

- Haven't got a bath? Dig through the cupboards and find a bowl large enough, or remind yourself next time you are in the shops to buy something suitable.

- If you're not keen on the idea of bathing your feet, you could simply give them a firm massage instead. Why not invest in some nice oil or lotion for them? If you want to go high-tech with this distraction, look into buying a foot massager. Whether it's a manual wooden one which you roll your feet over, or an electric all singing and dancing version; your feet will thank you for it.

FREE TO

54 : SMOOTH AS EVER

When I was fifteen and at the peak of my self-harming years, you might be surprised to learn that I still cared about not having stubbly legs in the summer. I know it might come as a surprise to some people; to hear that someone who doesn't care about life should still bother with such mundane things, but it was actually extremely important for me to focus on them. I reached a point where I was almost becoming defined by my self-harming actions and losing my sense of self. Ironically, the simple act of epilating my legs both helped me feel 'normal', and hurt so much that it was almost a socially acceptable method of self-harm: one which gave me fantastically smooth results.

Hair removal can be a great distraction and is often extremely satisfying; especially when it is something that we all have to do. Taking the time to pamper ourselves in this way is good for the soul, and doesn't have to be confined to our usual ablution hour. If it's midnight and you need a way to distract yourself; shave your legs. It doesn't matter that no-one will see them. The feel of fresh crisp sheets against newly shaved legs is worth it. Most importantly, if it helps you right now then this is all the reason you need.

Quick Tip

- If you normally shave with a razor, try something different and give hair removal cream or wax a go. If you are feeling really brave, then invest in an epilator and prepare yourself to pluck those pesky hairs away in great clumps.

- Take the time make yourself feel pampered. Perhaps you could make an evening of it and combine this shaving ritual with a nice hot bath, a refreshing face-mask, and a glass of your favourite drink (no electric shavers in the bath please!) Getting rid of unwanted hair doesn't have to be tedious.

- And boys, this isn't just a 'girl thing'. It could be time you bought a new set of blades for that razor, or treated yourself to some luxurious shaving oil, cream or gel. Next time you need a distraction, why not take it out on that stubble - carefully.

FREE

55 : YOU MUST HAVE A CLUBCARD FOR THAT

Every now and again when I am writing about something very personal to me, I stop and wonder 'am I the only one?' I worry that my honesty will reveal me as more than a little bit strange, and I fear that people simply won't be able to understand. This is one of those times.

The truth is, I love going to supermarkets.

A trip to Tesco has on more than one occasion served as an escape from depression; and a very good one at that. You don't even have to actually need something from the supermarket to make use of this distraction. Chances are you will probably come home with some items that caught your eye, but you could just as easily return home empty handed and the trip will have served its purpose.

Meandering down the aisles looking at all the weird and wonderful ingredients on offer can actually be quite inspiring, especially if you are on the look out for some cooking ideas. (See distraction number 2.) Whilst everyone else frog-marches their trolleys up and down; desperate to spend their money as quickly as possible before the queues build up, it can be satisfying to know that there is nothing you need except some time away from it all.

It sounds strange doesn't it? - To think of Sainsbury's as somewhere to go for a break. I'm sitting here hoping that at least someone else out there knows what I mean!

Just as stepping outside for some fresh air can be integral to the direction a heated discussion heads in, a quick 'pop to the shops' can work wonders. I've been in arguments that were destined to lead me towards self-harm, but I've managed to turn it around by choosing that exact moment to go and pick up some milk instead.

Quick Tip

- Make a note of your nearest supermarkets and their opening hours. The 24hr ones are perfect for this distraction, as we all know depressive thoughts don't work on a 9-5 schedule.

- If you feel like you would benefit by having something to focus on whilst in the shop, look for special offers or ways to get extra clubcard rewards. Often people earn enough loyalty points to use against things that could also act as excellent distractions. Restaurant deals, days out, or even holidays all feature in this book, and they can all be bought with clubcard points. Points really do mean prizes.

- Every time you discover something that you need to pick up on your next shopping trip, write it down on a list. If you don't feel happy going to the supermarket without buying something; grab the list on your way out. Remember to keep it somewhere easily accessible; ready for when you need this distraction. Ours is a magnetic notepad attached to the fridge.

This, like all distractions in this book, is about doing something else at the exact moment you realise that your mind is starting to hold onto negative thoughts. I'm not implying that a buy-one-get-one-free offer is everything you need to survive, but choosing to distract yourself from your demons is the best, and often hardest thing you can do.

FREE

56 : ENJOY THE SILENCE

This is a distraction that won't suit everyone, but you should be able to easily decide if it is one for you.

Just as music can be a positive distraction to lift your mood and calm you, so too can the absence of it. Our lives are filled with noise whether we like it or not, yet most of us rarely allow ourselves the time to enjoy the sound of silence.

To bathe in quietness - and I mean to truly cut out all the noise, our minds are allowed that space to simply exist calmly. The sound of your breath and heartbeat can be extremely peaceful if you can find a way to relax and listen.

It sounds easy doesn't it? I truly appreciate that in actual fact, finding benefits in silence can be rather difficult. Sometimes we can't simply switch off, and the lack of noise can aggravate feelings of anger or frustration.

I used to find that on some days it was impossible to escape my own self-destructive thoughts when everything around me was quiet, yet on other days; silence felt like a soothing arm around me.

Quick Tip

- Turn off the stereo, radio or television, and try sitting quietly for a moment. Try to not think about anything at all and concentrate only on your breathing. Close your eyes if you find that it helps: it usually does. Breathe in through you nose, and out through your mouth -

taking long, deep breaths. Let the sound of nothing soothe and relax you.

- It might be worth investing in some earplugs to help cut out external noise; especially if you live somewhere where background noise never leaves you.

- Teach yourself to meditate. Remember that meditation is not just about sitting quietly.

- Although I'm not a religious person, you might use this quiet time as an opportunity to lose yourself in prayer.

FREE TO

57 : WHAT WAS THAT FILM AGAIN?

We all have an all-time favourite film. You know; one that you could happily watch over and over again yet still never bore of. Mine is 'The Labyrinth' with David Bowie and Jennifer Connelly, and it doesn't matter how many times I see it, this film always brings a smile to my face.

That's just one of the fabulous things about great movies: you can usually watch them more than once and they will keep giving you enjoyment. With televisions in the home getting bigger and better, these days you don't even have to go to the cinema to be wowed.

Watching films is also a great excuse to be sociable, and it can sometimes be refreshing to know that you have an opportunity to see friends without anyone expecting conversation from you. Sometimes the last thing we feel like doing is talking, and so this is a perfect middle ground.

Every week Mike, Paul, and I have a film night where we order take-away food and watch classic films from our childhood. It's been great re-watching films that we haven't seen for years, and also seeing others for the first time. It's always good fun to sit and chat about how rubbish the effects are, or which ones we are going to watch next, and naturally it's just nice to see our friend as well.

Quick Tip

- An obvious suggestion when it comes to films is to get yourself down to the cinema - and this is the only reason the cost rating on this distraction went up! The cinema can be quite expensive, but I must admit that there are some films, which simply work better on the big screen.

- Why not dedicate an evening in the week to be film night? Having a set plan every week gives us a better perspective on time, and can also help us have something to look forward to. Just like me, you could resurrect some of those long forgotten ones and remind yourself why you loved, or even hated them.

- If you haven't already got a decent movie collection to pick from when you need this distraction, DVD's are getting cheaper and cheaper so you have no excuses not to stock up. For even better deals, you can also look at buying them second-hand.

- If you'd rather not buy films to watch (perhaps you haven't the storage space?), see if you can borrow a few from someone else, or perhaps rent them. There are rental companies where you can pick films online and then they post them out to you for a monthly flat fee, so you don't even need to leave the house.

58 : BLOW AWAY THE DUST

Living in a dirty, dusty home can be more depressing than we actually realise. I'm a firm believer that 'home' should be somewhere we are comfortable; a place we look forward to returning to. As the door to our abode opens; inviting us into a corridor of dead spiders and a living room that has changed colour under the layer of dust, if the first thought we have is 'oh', then this isn't going to make for the best state of mind.

Trust me: I'm not a clean-freak. Our house has a fair amount of mess and we don't tidy as often as we perhaps should (a clean house is the sign of a wasted life, right?) but despite this, I still see the benefits in making sure our homes are nice. Thus, cleaning the house makes an excellent distraction and has one added bonus: next time you have visitors; you won't be too ashamed to let them use the toilet.

Quick Tip

- Grab the Hoover, make sure the dust bag is ready for you and the vents are nice and clear, then get to work. Vacuum to your heart's content; even if you end up going over the same spot twice. If your Hoover is anything like ours, you'll be sweating with exhaustion at the end and will be just about ready for bed.

- There are many other ways to clean the house, which equally act as great ways to stop your mind from dwelling. Now is the right time to wipe down the kitchen counters, clean out the oven, scrub the bath and toilet, and dust those annoying cubbyholes.

- If you haven't already got a cupboard full of various lotions and potions for killing bacteria and banishing limescale, take a trip to the supermarket and see what's on offer. Maybe you can combine this distraction with number 11 and take this opportunity to use more eco-friendly cleaning solutions.

Whilst cleaning doesn't sound like the most exciting of distractions, it truly can be a great thing. When you can physically see and smell the difference you have made from scrubbing away, you'll most likely find yourself feeling quite satisfied. This is a darn site better than feeling the curse of your soul-destroyer. The people who live with you will probably agree!

FREE

59 : PLAY IN THE PARK

We are lucky enough to live opposite one of the gates to a big park. Whilst it is often so tempting to stay indoors, curl up and feel miserable, it is usually much more beneficial to try and get outside. Fresh air is so important for keeping our minds healthy and can often help us think more clearly. I even wrote most of my first book in this very park near home, as I found it so much easier to write with the sun shining down on me - with only the deer sniffing my bike for company.

The great thing about parks is there is so much you can do in them. You might simply chose to go for a long walk or cycle, but how about distracting yourself by taking the dog for a walk or playing Frisbee. If you can get a group of friends together, maybe it's time to have a game of football or cricket with them.

If you're not sure where you local park or green space is, have a look at a map and hunt one down. Don't be put off if it's not quite walking distance away; perhaps you can cycle or drive there?

Quick Tip

- If you need a distraction quickly and don't have time to get a group of people together, why not go for a walk, run, or cycle in the park. Or perhaps take the dog out. I'm sure your canine friend won't complain at the extra exercise.

- Playing Frisbee, cricket, football, or a simple game of catch can be really good fun if you have others to play with. If you decide to try some of the circus arts (see distraction number 93), many of these can be done outside also. My friend and I spent quite a few evenings juggling glowing balls or spinning glowing poi in the park at night, and have had great fun on the unicycle on a sunny Saturday afternoon.

- If it happens to be snowing right now, how long has it been since you built a snowman or went sledging? I bought myself a cheap plastic sledge at the end of last winter; ready for next time, after I realised just how much fun I could be having on that simple slope near work. I nearly always find that as much as I don't feel like stepping outside in the cold, once I'm wrapped up and out there, I'm pleased I made the effort. Rolling a giant ball of snow into a snow beast took me right back to my carefree childhood, and I also enjoyed the chance to take some wintery photographs. Even if you don't feel as though you can be bothered, or believe that the outside world is far too cold - play in the park anyway. Just think how nice it will be when you return to a lovely warm home and a cup of tea!

FREE TO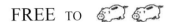

60 : BUY A PUNCH-BALL

This is quite an obvious one really. If you are feeling angry or frustrated and your emotions are bubbling away in there; tempting you to lash out: possibly on yourself, letting it out on a punch-ball is far more constructive than finding yourself with bruised knuckles, a hole in the wall, or fresh cuts on your body.

Exercise; as I keep mentioning, is an excellent tool because the chemical reaction in your body acts as a natural remedy for depression. Ironically however, exercise is often the last thing we envisage ourselves doing when everything around us seems crap. But this is the very way that you will beat this feeling. If you can try doing something different; no matter how much your brain is telling you not to bother, you will be making the very first step towards helping yourself.

I bought myself a punch-ball along with a mini trampoline when they were both discounted in the high street. I never really pictured myself using either, but my housemate encouraged me to set them up, and the two of us happily punched and kicked away until it was time for dinner. It felt great! I hit that blue and grey striped ball whilst depression simmered then boiled away from me, and she took swings at it as if it were the head of the ex-boyfriend who plagued her mind.

Quick Tip

- Punch-balls are an excellent way to vent misguided anger and relieve stress, and are not just for trainee boxers. They can be floor standing, wall or ceiling mounted, and are great to have set up for those unexpected times when you need this distraction.

- As already mentioned in the self-harm quick tips, punching cushions or soft toys can be just as effective, although cannot so easily be passed-off as a form of exercise. Outsiders are often fearful of expressions of anger such as this, so it really would be an idea to invest in a punch-ball if you plan on using this distraction often.

FREE

61 : PUT ON YOUR WALKING BOOTS
(COMFY SHOES WILL DO)

I've always been a firm believer that there is nothing quite like being outside in the fresh air. The benefits of natural light, exercise and leading a healthy lifestyle in general have already been mentioned in other chapters in this book, but I feel that walking deserves a page of its own.

The beauty of something as simple as going for a walk is that we all know how to do it, and it always costs nothing. It might be a cliché that people are often told to 'go for a walk and come back when you've calmed down', but like all clichés, statements like this exist for a reason.

There have been times when I have felt so depressed that it were as if I was physically unable to think or speak. I have curled up against a pillow soaked from my tears, completely unable to explain what I felt or why, which in turn has made me feel worse. It can be hard for others to understand what this helplessness is really like unless they have been in that position themselves, but it should be easy to appreciate that only the simple actions will get through such a heavy, depressive fog.

When everything seems to be too much effort, walking can be the one little lifeline that reaches us. If I could apply just one distraction to all forms of soul-destroyers and be sure that it would yield even a tiny positive reaction, this would be it. This might sound like a lot to place on such a simple action, but its simplicity is exactly why it is so perfect. Whether you feel angry, upset, desperate, worthless, depressed or unloved; I urge you to walk.

Going for a walk often gives us the opportunity to step away from a situation that might be contributing to our mood, and sometimes we don't even realise that it is. Whether taking a break from our office to walk, or escaping things at home - we all need times where we can remove ourselves from our surroundings and allow our minds to filter without the clutter of daily life. The physical exertion can help some emotions dissipate throughout us. (I've often walked so vigorously that the urge to cut myself has bubbled throughout my body and vanished by the time I've returned home, even though my mind still expected to self-harm.)

Whilst it can be useful to set specific time aside to get out, remember that you don't always need to plan to take a walk. Mike and I were about to head to a pub in the next town for Sunday lunch when it dawned on me that instead of driving, we could walk through the park to get there. I had been having a particularly stressful and emotional few weeks, and whilst the thought of driving there didn't consciously bother me, it wasn't until I had the grass under my bare feet and the sun shining on my head that I realised I was extremely pleased we weren't in the car.

I wouldn't have said that our original plan would have made me feel worse, but this tiny last minute change made everything seem surprisingly easier to cope with. The following evening I returned from work and made up a simple excuse for us to go for a walk, and again found myself soothed and distracted by the break in our routine.

Quick Tip

- If you had to pick just one distraction to try at your most needy of times, make it walking.

- If you are worried about where you might end up if left to your own devices, walk with someone else. You'll probably find that most people need an excuse to get out, and it shouldn't be too hard to give them that push. Going for a walk is one of the least intrusive things you can ask of someone, and can be tailored to fit into any amount of time you have to spare.

- Often we need that extra boost of encouragement, so give yourself a reason to go walking. Does the dog need to go out? Maybe your neighbour's dog would like someone new to trot beside. Or maybe you simply need a pint of milk, or could buy tomorrows lunch now to save time later.

- If you'd rather plan some time on your feet, take a look at a map and see what area takes your fancy. Maybe there is a park, forest or woodlands nearby that you've never noticed before, or a museum you could wander around for a while if the weather isn't adding to the appeal of being outside. It wouldn't defeat the point if you even had to drive or get public transport to somewhere that you could then go walking.

Whether you are only able to walk for five minutes right now, or have time to keep going until your energy runs out, don't believe those thoughts telling you it's not worth it. Even if you can't see the benefits yourself immediately, have faith that they do exist. Walking won't be a miracle cure, but it is that tiny step towards a more positive outlook; no pun intended.

Sophia Gill

FREE

62 : SET A GOAL

Having a specific goal in mind might sound ridiculously simple and obvious, but it is often something that many of us fail to do. There have been many times in my life when if I think back, I've basically been drifting along aimlessly. I might have felt happy on a shallow level, but deep down I firmly believe that we do need goals in order to remain strong.

Having a long-term goal (or two) helps us to feel focussed; even on a subconscious level, and this focus can be utilised as strength to fight. As a very basic example, I have a target in mind to be even just a little more toned when I get married next year; which is a goal born from the idea that I want to feel confident at our beach wedding in front of our closest family and friends. This tiny thought in the back of my mind is what helps me to jump on the exercise bike; even if I'm craving a comfy sofa and a bag of crisps, and helps me to believe that there is still purpose. My goal stops me from wallowing in a lack of self-confidence and gives me strength to quite literally ride out the negative feelings.

I also have a goal to be published, and this extremely strong desire is what encourages me to keep writing. It helps me strive for perfection and demands that I beat away those moments when I doubt my future. Without this very definite goal I might perhaps never have written this book, and would possibly have never taking writing seriously. Whichever way I look at it, whether I've succeeded in this goal or not; not even trying to aim would have been a much bigger disaster as writing has been my very method of coping.

Without goals, it is all too easy for depression to convince us that there is nothing in life to live for. The negative thoughts find it much harder to battle against you if you can begin to understand exactly where you are now, and where you are heading in the future; because you will be more willing to accept that these negative feelings are transient. Goals put our lives into much better perspective and can reward us with that important sense of achievement. Better still, often we find that working towards something specific is rewarding enough; even if we perhaps have to move the goalposts along the way. This means that you don't even have to fully reach that initial goal in order for this distraction to be beneficial - it's often the actual act of setting a goal that is important.

Quick Tip

- Think about what you would like to achieve in life and then try and set yourself at least one long-term goal. This isn't just about creating a to-do-list; this is about having something specific to aim for. It doesn't matter how silly each goal might sound in principle; as long as it gives you something to work towards. Perhaps there is a salary or ideal job that you'd like to aim for, or maybe a future without something such as self-harm, alcohol or cigarettes? Are you keen to change your diet, lose weight or simply tone up? Whatever works for you; try and remain realistic. There is no point setting a goal so high that even thinking about it depresses you. Keep in mind that these goals should inspire you. Next time you find yourself with a choice to make, consider each goal carefully and decide if any of your options will affect your future plans, or perhaps take you one step closer.

- If you think it might help you to stay focussed, write your goals down and put them somewhere where you can be reminded of each one. Let them spur you on along the journey, and don't be afraid to adjust a goal if it no longer feels quite right. It's not cheating or failing; it's learning that ideas and values often change, and thus our goals sometimes need to be re-adjusted.

- Perhaps you would benefit from keeping some form of record of your progress? For example, when trying to lose weight it can be helpful to see a chart of the weight loss each day; to remind you that your plan is working. This is especially important when progress is slow and steady over time, as often we can become bogged down by the wait. Let yourself feel fulfilled by every step of your progress, and use this record to inspire you at times when the future feels hazy.

- Equally as important as setting long-term goals, you should also think about how you can break those plans down into more maneagble chunks. Using a diet as an example again, you might want to eventually lose a few stone but your objective on a daily basis could be to lose a few pounds each week. Having short-term goals that still lead to the same overall goal can help you to feel a sense of accomplishment in your daily life, whilst keeping you motivated towards the future.

Sophia Gill

LONG-TERM DISTRACTIONS

It is an excellent start to use short-term distractions as a way of avoiding negative emotions; such as tormenting yourself about a failed relationship, or indulging in destructive behaviour like self-harm - but this is only part of the healing process.

Long-term distractions are about having plans and goals for the future - even if to you that simply means tomorrow; because having this focus is important in creating a healthy and happier environment.

There is a big difference between plodding along feeling satisfied with the world, and feeling as though your life is totally empty and thus you truly have no reason to be alive. These feelings are what separate a 'normal' person from someone suffering from depression, but it is also fair to say that everyone will have their moments of despair at some time or another.

I believe that a big part of how we cope with the inevitable difficulties is to do with the support structure that we have created for ourselves, and how we have trained our minds to deal with the things that are thrown at us. The ideas in the second-half of this book are to help you introduce methods of coping via means that are not simply about the here and now; because they require a little bit of forethought. This, in essence, is teaching you to build your own support structure; equipping you for times when you might need it to hold you up.

As always, these next thirty-nine distractions are also here to introduce you to things that you may never have considered; in the hope that you may even discover a new passion. Depression hates it when we try new things -

because it might mean that we find ourselves too busy to listen to those negative thoughts. Of course being busy alone isn't going to fight the illness, but focus and enjoyment help us to form moments where we can think with clarity. This leads to a much better understanding of what has caused the feelings that we are experiencing, and therefore to an idea of how to move past them.

Long-term distractions may require more energy than the short-term ones, but you must believe that this is energy that you will find. It may not be immediate, but the beauty in all 101 distractions is that they are designed to be used whenever they best suit you.

FREE

63 : PLAN IT

The thought of planning can send shivers down some people's spines, but for those of us needing ways to escape the suffocating negative thoughts, this can be a surprisingly good distraction.

Often we find ourselves stuck in the same routine, lasting days, weeks or even years. Before we know it we're sat at the table eating Christmas dinner, wondering what happened and what we've done with the past year.

Breaking that routine is healthy because it can give us things to look forward to, and reminds us that there can be moments we recall with pleasure. Personally I find that making a plan means I am much more likely to find the energy to stick to it, whereas if I let myself 'see what I feel like on the day', I'll probably end up sat doing nothing.

One of my favourite types of plan is to take advantage of special offers, often spending one or two nights away from home. I've stayed in hotels only half an hour from my house, just to see somewhere new and feel like I've had a mini break. Whereas most people wouldn't think to pay money to sleep so close to home, they could be missing out on a chance to see the area from a different perspective.

Not once have we regretted our mini-trips, and most of them have cost less than an hours wage (and no, we are not exactly top earners!) Attracted by a very cheap hotel room, we've seen parts of the country that we would never have thought to visit ordinarily.

If you'd rather not spend anything at all, why not create a plan for the weekend. Maybe there is a new recipe you've been meaning to try, or a walk that someone has recommended you go on? Most of us always have things that need doing around the house. Perhaps you can decide to tackle one of those? Whatever it is that you think you'd like to do, making a plan for it might be that little push you need.

Quick Tip

- Is someone close to you about to have a birthday? This year you could make it one to remember by planning a surprise for them. Or maybe you could work on a treasure hunt that leads to their present. Planning doesn't have to be tedious. If you get creative with it, sometimes the planning can be equally fun.

- If travelling isn't really your thing, or you'd rather leave the holiday arrangements to an agent, why not plan a day trip instead. Perhaps there is a museum you've always wanted to visit, or show you want to see. Decide to make a day of it and think about places you can meet, have a coffee, or refuel with a nice meal. Maybe there is a good deal on a hotel nearby and you can treat yourself to an evening away.

Having plans each week; no matter how simple, can help you focus on the good things in your life; leaving you less time to dwell on the negatives. Because depression feels endless, planning things that segment each week makes it easier to feel like you are coping. Sometimes it is necessary to separate one week from the next so that you can focus on that smaller chunk of life, instead of being daunted by the endless future.

64 : PICK YOUR OWN

Very few of us in this world truly have a chance to display our hunter-gatherer natural instincts, and personally I worry that the further we remove ourselves from the natural world the more problems we end up creating. I don't mean that in order to be happy you need to clamber up your neighbour's apple tree wearing animal fur, holding a bone-shaped baton. It's more about tuning into nature to help rid us from unnecessary stress, and create a moment in time where we have a chance to feel that our lives are worthwhile.

I don't know if you agree, but there is something rather clinical about buying fruit and vegetables in neat, clean, perfect plastic packets. Worse still is that plonking a punnet of raspberries on the checkout then into our fridges ready to eat, isn't the most satisfying of feelings. It hardly helps us feel as though we have worked for this food, and often this means we simply take it for granted; leaving it to rot over weeks before consigning it to the recycling bin.

Removing ourselves from the satisfaction of 'earning' our food is, on a primitive level, closing the door to a tiny snippet of positive thought. Ultimately it comes down to the society that we live in today, but there is a chance to re-open that door and reap the rewards: find a farm to pick your own fruit and vegetables.

'Pick your own' was actually a form of therapy used by the psychiatric hospital I was a patient of as a teenager, and I cannot recommend this idea enough. Those of us allowed to go out (who had proved we were not a danger to ourselves or others) were taken strawberry picking at a nearby farm. I have photos from the occasion and look back on them to notice that

I have never seen so many happy faces on a bunch of very troubled people. We picked more strawberries than we knew what to do with, for the simple reason that picking them was both fun and rewarding. It hadn't even crossed our minds what we were actually going to do with six punnets full each.

Every time I have ever gone fruit and vegetable picking, I have made just that little bit more effort to ensure we use all of our fresh food. Not only do we waste less and enjoy more; we better appreciate that growing works in seasons, and this results in us trying food that we perhaps would overlook in the supermarket. Instead of buying food because it is 'buy one get one free', you are picking it because it is currently at its best.

It is always the little appreciations in life, which affect our state of mind in the long-term, and this is the key to building up your defences.

Quick Tip

- Ask around and see if any nearby farms offer 'pick your own' days. My parents always seemed to know the best ones near us and their exact costs, but this kind of information is also readily available online. If you need a distraction now and the farm happens to be open, then go. It doesn't matter what is currently in season. Even if you pick something to give away, it will get you out the house with a great purpose, and send you home with a sense of achievement.

- If the farm isn't open right now, then make a plan to try out this distraction another time. Perhaps you can see if your friends or family would also like to pass an afternoon picking fruit and vegetables? Often these kinds of things get forgotten about because we don't have someone else to go with, and not because we don't find it fun.

Don't let yourself be put off by excuses such as 'what would we do with all those fruits?' You could combine this with distraction number 2 or 39 and make something specifically to use up anything you pick and can't eat. Now might be the best time to try and make your own preserves, smoothies or fruit drinks. You might also spark a new passion for home-grown and hand-picked food, enough to start your own vegetable garden at home or in an allotment. (See distraction number 89.)

162

FREE (IF YOU ARE ALREADY A MEMBER)
TO

65 : VISIT OR JOIN

Lazy Sunday afternoons milling around the house doing absolutely nothing can be great; when you're not depressed. The main problem I have with the idea of not doing anything during our time off, is that days merge together and heighten those melancholic feelings of 'nothing ever changes.' You see, if it ever reaches a point when it is tricky to distinguish one day from another and this week from the next; then those feelings of a never-ending routine actually have a basic foundation to grow on.

I personally feel that life is about experiences: both good and bad. If we never go out and try new things then we lessen our chances of being able to learn from them. Often we make excuses based on our spare time or funds available, yet equally we often just lack motivation. Now is the time to be inspired to get out.

If there is a place local enough for you to consider visiting a few times a year, then it is worth look at becoming a member there. Mike and I are season ticket holders to Kew Gardens; which is only a ten-minute drive from our home, and also to the National Trust; 'because you are never more than forty minutes from a great day out.' We are quite proud of often being the youngest people at the entrance to some of our local National Trust places, and we have never once regretted visiting any of them. Sometimes we even plan weekends away based on which of their houses we can visit that are a little further from home; usually making the most of a special offer on a hotel so that our total trip costs next to nothing.

One of the things we love about our memberships to various places is that because I have already paid the money through a direct debit, we are far more inclined to 'make the most of it' by visiting somewhere at least enough times to claw-back the normal cost per day. For us, it makes planning a few hours out of the house just that little bit easier, and it doesn't matter if we change our mind and come home again. No money has exchanged hands on the day, and thus it doesn't feel as though we're losing anything.

For years we also had membership cards that allowed us to get into a number of theme parks across the UK; which was especially handy seeing as we live less than half an hour away from two of the biggest ones. There have been days when we've literally turned up at Thorpe Park, gone on our favourite ride once, decided we were bored of the crowds and driven home again. It was still excellent fun and I'm sure that if we didn't have the freedom of the passes, we simply would have sat at home feeling bored. As pitiful as this might sound, I believe it is fair to say that we all have days when we just can't think of anything to do. Getting out for an hour or two can make a great difference to our state of mind, and can help us to reign in some of those worsening emotions.

Naturally you don't have to become a member of somewhere to enjoy what it has to offer, and by all means do go even if you have to buy a ticket for the day. The only problem I find with spending money on entrance fees or pre-booking an afternoon visit is that you will naturally feel obliged to stick it out long enough in order to 'get your money's worth.' Membership cancels out this feeling; actually giving you much more freedom and greater satisfaction, and allows you the chance to be more spontaneous - something I love. It's also a wonderful feeling knowing that you can bypass the queue at the ticket desk and walk straight in; almost as if privy to a special club. I guess in some ways this is exactly what paying for membership is about, but I personally see it as one of the excellent tools against depression.

Quick Tip

- Have a look online and see what places of interest there are near you. Some have their own membership schemes; such as Kew Gardens or privately owned properties, but others allow you to join and visit a number of places all over the country. National Trust is excellent for this, along with The Royal Horticultural Society and English Heritage. Remember that membership schemes are not just limited to places that you might feel are only suited to your parents.

Some theme parks are grouped together to allow you to buy a pass for them all, whilst others have their own membership offer.

- If you are already participating in something like this, dig out your membership card and plan a visit. Often you can go there once a week and still feel as though you are seeing something new. Some days Mike and I head to Kew because we just fancy a walk, but other times we will pack a picnic or visit one of their exhibitions. Places will advertise special events throughout the year, so make sure to keep an eye on any newsletters they send you in the post or via email.

- If you can't justify spending cash on a membership fee, perhaps you have some loyalty points you can redeem instead? Supermarkets often have schemes that give you far better value for your points if you spend them on vouchers for days out or memberships like this. If you haven't quite got enough points yet, perhaps this is something you could work towards? Don't forget to give every member of your household their own clubcard to collect with so you don't miss out on opportunities to top up that all-important balance.

- Perhaps someone you know would appreciate you taking them out for the day? As members, I am posted special 'friends' rates or free tickets during the quieter season. My mum will always say yes to our suggestions to meet up, and often it is more fun to visit a place with someone who has never been there before.

Sophia Gill

FREE TO 🐷

66 : CAR-BOOT IT

You know I am my fathers daughter by the simple fact that I will get out of bed early on a Sunday morning to wander around a field full of unwanted clutter, while my stomach rumbles for breakfast. Little else can drag me out of bed at such unsocial hours; especially when it causes me to miss my peanut butter on toast.

Whilst the attraction of a car boot sale to me began purely as an opportunity to spend valuable time with my dad during his increasingly infrequent visits to the UK, I did quickly discover other benefits. Finding random objects of interest ignited my creative spark, and I would always return home eager to do something. Whether that be to move furniture around to make space for a surprise purchase, or dig out some ingredients to try recipes from a cookbook I'd acquired for 10p; car boot sales always inspired me.

From my experience, depression hates it when you ignore those calls to hibernate and instead get yourself out and about doing things. Although it may feel impossible to ever loosen that awful grip on you, distractions are a chance to deny negativity the chance to fester.

If for the only reason that you can never predict what you will find at a car boot, try and give this one a go. Positive things can spring from uncertainty, and at worst you can simply come home early and get back into bed.

Quick Tip

- Check your local newspapers to see if there are any car-boot sales in your area. They tend to only be on Sunday but you might find the odd one cropping up on other days. Many are advertised by signs outside the school or field that they are to be held, so keep your eyes peeled as you walk or drive around.

- Perhaps you can indulge your hobbies and interests at the next car boot, bric-a-brac or jumble sale. You might find that comic you've wanted for ages, or some cheap craft materials. I never cease to be amazed at what some people throw out. If you are worried about spending too much or bringing home more than you need, set yourself an allowance and be sure to stick to it.

- If you've tackled distraction number 51 you'll probably be in an excellent position to sell those unwanted items at a car boot sale. Getting rid of clutter is extremely therapeutic, and it's a bonus if you earn some money while you do it. Don't fool yourself into thinking 'but no one will want this old...' You'll be surprised what people buy! It might feel like junk to you, but it's another man's treasure - so the saying goes.

FREE

67 : GET PAID

Once I finally accepted that I needed to start hauling myself out of debt, I started doing I.T. support work in my evenings and weekends in order to raise some extra cash. My friend and I braced the cold, dark winter nights, and stumbled across paths blocked by spider webs and slippery wet leaves in order to post leaflets through the doors of local residents. Just the leaflet drop alone was actually a pretty good distraction because we managed to make it into something quite fun - using it as an excuse to get outside and have a good natter. We certainly welcomed a cosy living room and a cup of tea afterwards.

I found myself feeling quite nervous and reluctant to answer my phone once I knew that I'd put myself out there - even though I was getting the exact response we had hoped for. I've always found it hard to appreciate my skills in the I.T. world, despite having worked in this field for well over a decade. I somehow felt not worthy of being paid to help strangers, and I became terrified of failure.

However, once I managed to get over the initial fear and made a commitment to take a look at the endless virus and pop-up problems, I actually found that I really enjoyed my part-time work. As expected, the problems I was called to help out with formed the sort of work I could do with my eyes closed, and this quickly proved to my negative mind that I had nothing to worry about. Not only did it help me to appreciate my work and accept that I did actually hold some useful knowledge, I also found that I started to enjoy my day job more too.

Sophia Gill

This distraction worked absolute wonders for me because it totally rebuilt my feeling of self-worth and gave me a rocket boost in confidence. So much so, that the extra money jingling around in my pocket became almost inconsequential. Whereas perhaps in my nine to five job I would have months go by without any form of satisfaction or feeling that I was indeed needed, in just an hour helping someone at their home, I could last for ages feeling like a saviour. In fact, I reckon you would have even seen a skip in my step as I walked home.

Quick Tip

- Think carefully about whether or not there is skill or hobby that you could earn from. We're not talking about career changing decisions; just something that you could do now and again to make a bit of pocket money. It might be that you could teach others a language, instrument or how to do something such as fix their computer or plumbing. Or perhaps you enjoy making things that could be sold at craft fairs or via the Internet. We often take our own talents for granted and this distraction is fantastic when we need help opening our eyes to see our strengths.

If you are feeling rather uninspired, remind yourself that there is so much more to gain here than a bit of extra cash. It is an amazing feeling to know that you are able to help someone, so if you do posses a certain skill, don't be afraid to share it. You can also meet some very interesting people while doing part-time work, and you never know what other doors this may open for you.

FREE to

68 : YOU ARE CORDIALLY INVITED

Speaking to other people who have also suffered with depression, it seems to be that in the process of trying to cope we often cut people off and push loved ones away. It's almost an automatic response.

I know that I subconsciously poisoned relationships; partially because I didn't see the point when in the back of my mind I planned suicide, but also because I just didn't think I was worthy of the love and affection. I'd convinced myself that friends only wanted to spend time with me because they felt guilty; as if they had a duty to uphold - despite the fact there was no evidence to actually support this.

Engaging your friends and family during these difficult emotions is one of the best things you can do, as no one should have to fight alone. Apart from not avoiding social events such as trips to the pub, cinema or similar, perhaps you could organise a party to get everyone together for some fun.

Quick Tip

- A party doesn't have to be a grand and glorious affair; it can simply be a chance for you and your close friends to enjoy a meal together. Something like a dinner party gives you a goal to focus on, and offers opportunity to show off your cooking skills. If you don't feel confident that you can send your guests home without upset stomachs, perhaps you could arrange an event where everyone brings a dish of food or some drinks? You could allocate each person a specific course to provide; such as starter, main, or desert; whether it's home-cooked or bought.

- Perhaps you could hold a themed party, and invite your guests to get involved by coming in fancy dress. Dressing up is often something that we haven't done since childhood, even though it can be excellent fun. If you give your costume 100% effort, you'll end up feeling much more confident in it; and not just like the person who grabbed a cheap last-minute mask from a petrol station on the way to a Halloween party.

- Have a think about the kind of party you know your friends would enjoy. I know that some of our friends are not as keen on fancy dress as I am, but would be much more excited by the thought of a murder mystery party. Kits are readily available online, and allow you to get as involved as you want to. Again, if you throw caution to the wind and make the effort to really get into the swing of it, usually others will follow. It might feel a bit out of your comfort zone at first, but once you start to relax and enjoy yourself, you can go to sleep that night feeling happy that you and your friends have had a nice time. This naturally helps people to bond, and the importance of this becomes very apparent in times of need.

- If organising a party really is too much for you to think about right now, at very least you should try and ensure that you accept any invitations that come your way. I've forced myself to attend parties even though all I really wanted was to curl up at home and weep. Despite perhaps feeling exposed and uncomfortable at first, I've left with the realisation that it actually wasn't that bad; like I'd had fun even. The point is, by not going to social events you've already closed the door on an opportunity to feel better; even if you don't believe it possible. Up your chances by going anyway; at very least it will get you out of the house for a few hours.

FREE

69 : VISIT YOUR LIBRARY

Libraries can be extremely soothing places, and if all those books aren't enough of a reason for you to visit, why not simply head to your local library for some peace and quiet.

When I was just starting to really suffer with depression I found it extremely helpful to know that I could retreat to the town library and sit quietly to do my homework. It meant that I could avoid being at home when things were difficult, yet still be in a safe and secure environment where it wasn't possible for me to self-harm.

Just knowing I had 'somewhere to go' was actually enough to release some of the pressure that I felt; even if I didn't always utilise it. That is, I often didn't have to be in the library to feel comforted by the knowledge of it.

On another note, I also found it quite satisfying to borrow things from my library; knowing that they had to be returned by a certain date. I tended to find that I was more likely to read those borrowed books than if I had just bought them; and this meant that I was not only reading more overall during my depression, but I was saving money too.

Quick Tip

- If you've never been to the library or haven't been since you were at school, now is the time to join or re-join. Find one close to either your home or work and ask them about membership. Take a slow wander around and let your eyes browse the shelves. You might find a book catches your eye, which you never would have found otherwise. Remember that you don't have to be actively on the hunt for a specific book in order to return home with one. Sometimes loitering without intent is the best way to discover new titles.

- If you're not interested in borrowing books, remember that some libraries also have films or music that can be loaned. They are often much cheaper than rental stores, although they probably won't have all the latest releases. Your local library might also have a computer with Internet access; which might be useful if you need some time away from home but don't want to disconnect completely.

- Why not sit quietly and read in the library, or perhaps use the time as an opportunity to work? Some people find that they are better able to concentrate without homely distractions such as children, parents, pets, or phonecalls. You might find that the library is the perfect environment to be inspired. Just remember to turn your mobile on silent.

FREE TO

70 : BE A TOURIST

I have lived in the outskirts of London for my whole life, and yet most tourists have seen more of the sights than I have. Don't get me wrong; I absolutely love to travel and see new things, but I automatically think of trips much further afield. And this is often the way with the country we live in - we don't think to visit the typical tourist sights or arrange day trips to admire the places so close to home. Now is the time to be a tourist in your own country!

My idea of a holiday used to naturally mean getting on a plane and travelling abroad, but more recently I've discovered that it can be great to experience the UK through the eyes of a foreigner. Whereas in the past I would walk past London tours with a quickening pace; trying to avoid the crowd of people taking weird holiday snaps, I've learnt to pause and ask myself whether this is one tour I should go on someday.

Quick Tip

- Think about what attractions or tours people would do if they were visiting your area, and plan to do them yourself. If tourists are a rarity near your hometown, think instead about the next big city close by, and arrange a visit. Ignore the fact that it might feel strange to you. The idea is to see the places you take for granted in a different light.

- Why not hop on tour bus, join a boat trip, or find a walking tour you can take part in? It can be fun to have a guide explain the history of the place, and you might even learn something new.

- Have you ever seen the museums near you? Perhaps the last time you went to them was as a child. Now is the perfect time to see how much has changed. Perhaps there is a special exhibition that interests you; which won't be around forever.

- Once you've exhausted the tourist spots nearby, its time to plan a longer trip to see other parts of the country. The possibilities are endless.

The great thing about this distraction is that when you start to learn about your hometown and country, it can help you feel more grounded. I never felt as though I particularly belonged anywhere and have certainly never felt even the slightest bit patriotic, but as I started seeing and learning about all the better things in the UK, it made me appreciate 'home'.

Coming back from another country, I used to suffer badly with post-holiday depression, and whilst I still have more than the average urge to travel in order to keep me sane, I can now cope with returning to normality. This is largely because I appreciate there is still so much for me to see in the UK, and thus the end of a holiday doesn't have to mean slotting back into a mundane life.

FREE TO 🐹🐹

71 : PUSH THE BOAT OUT

When I was a much smaller girl than I am now, my parents would pack a wonderful picnic on a nice sunny day and then hire a rowboat to sail us down the Thames. I remember begging my mum to let me dip my feet in the water, and secretly hoped that my dad would row us under a weeping willow tree so that we could pretend we had floated into a magical land.

Although I'm not what I would consider to be a friend of water, there is something very refreshing about drifting down the river while you leave those worries moored up to entertain themselves on land.

A friend and I even became so fascinated with the river that we bought two cheap inflatable one-person kayaks; along with various accessories to prepare us for all eventualities. If we should ever find ourselves capsized and stranded on a desert island, we would surely cope!

I would come home from work feeling depressed and frustrated, and he would drag me down to the Thames with our boats on the back seat. Often we would paddle until our arms hurt, but no matter how long we spent on the water; we would always dry ourselves off in agreement that 'we should so do that more often.'

Those kayaking days happened to be during a particularly difficult redundancy threat at work, and whilst I was in a terrible relationship with a cheating bully. Consequently, I must admit to having flirted with self-harm again, yet it never became the serious addiction that it once was. Despite those challenging times, our outings made me feel strong and happier in myself and diffused the negative emotions that had built up during my working day. Combined with many other distractions that I also used during this time, I managed to wade through emotions that I was convinced would never leave me.

Quick Tip

- Why not head down to your nearest lake, river or sea, and work some muscles by hiring a rowboat. Some places may have a kayak, canoe or pedalo to rent if you prefer; all of which can take your mind of your difficulties. If you want to make more of a day of it, pack a picnic to enjoy while you are out.

- If you'd rather not get involved with the actual rowing part, perhaps there is a boat tour that you could join. Being on the water gives you a totally different viewpoint so don't be putt-off doing tours in your local area. They can be just as interesting as the type of tours we do whilst on holiday.

- Although in a completely different league, you might enjoy heading down to your nearest expanse of water to play around with a remote controlled boat. They can be great fun and far less tiring, plus you don't need quite as much water. Perhaps there is a pond nearby that you can race around in? Just a small word of advice though: make sure your toy doesn't run out of charge right in the middle. You don't want to have to wade out to rescue it!

FREE to

72 : HIT THE SHOPS

As much as we reluctantly have to admit it: happiness cannot be bought for any price. However, there is something quite therapeutic about shopping and it makes for a great explanation as to why I ended up in so much debt (It's my feeble excuse and I'm sticking to it!)

I'm not sure if it is a gender thing (most men I know seem to go into an anti-shopping trance when faced with a shopping centre) but us girls do seem to like to shop, and anything that some of us enjoy doing is worthy of being in this book.

I remember when I was really just starting to tackle depression I used shopping as a way to try and comfort myself. Clothes especially became my hope to look at myself with more forgiving eyes, when all I knew was complete lack in self-confidence. I recall feeling quite excited when I introduced a single yellow tee shirt into a wardrobe full of black and grey clothing; almost as if this slither of colour represented my hidden positive side.

Books were my other fascination and I often shopped for them purely so that I could know I always had one more unread book waiting to distract me. What I perhaps failed to notice until now however, was that the actual act of meandering in and out of shops carefree was also something which kept me from self-harm, and gave me much-needed breathing space from my mental illness.

Naturally we all have to keep control over our spending, but as already mentioned, this distraction isn't about parting with tonnes of money in the hope of buying happiness. Allow yourself to be treated occasionally, but also remember that you can go shopping purely to take your mind off things. This can be just as successful if you come home empty handed.

Quick Tip

- Whilst I do see the sadness of living in such a materialistic society, I do think it is important to treat ourselves once in a while; and often this will mean buying that coat we always wanted or a new CD to listen to in the car. Maybe you could set yourself a budget to spend in the shops as a reward for not self-harming?

- One of the many wondrous things about the Internet is that we are now able to make purchases from the comfort of our soft leather sofa, whilst sipping on a lovely cup of tea. Another bonus is that online shopping can be done at any time of day or night, making this the type of distraction that can also be used in the short-term. See if you can do some of your shopping online, but whatever you do, remember to keep your card details safe. Only buy from trusted sites and never send your card number via email.

- If you know that you would find it therapeutic to opt for the more traditional method of shopping, then allow yourself the time to wander around the high street or shopping centre. Remember you don't have to buy anything and could just as easily be distracted by doing some window-shopping.

- Why not set yourself a task to look for that birthday or Christmas present early, or try to hunt out the best bargains. My friends and I once went shopping with the mission to pick out the most horrible clothes we could find. Although we had no intention of making a purchase, we had a great laugh trying everything on and giggling over how silly we looked.

FREE TO

73 : START LEARNING

Personally, I believe that learning is one of the most important things that we can do in our lives. If we cease to learn, we quickly become stale and find ourselves wondering about our purpose. It's not just about keeping up with your place of work so that you can use the latest technology or 'talk the talk'. Learning is what makes us unique and interesting, and we may just surprise ourselves with the things we know. (See distraction number 49.)

In my very early years with depression I made myself a promise that I wouldn't visit Egypt; a place I was fascinated with, until I had taught myself to read hieroglyphs - not the usual 17-year-old's hobby I must admit. Now I can be extremely tough on myself, and so my passion for ancient Egyptian history inadvertently gave me a very definite goal and a reason to fight the negative drivel in my mind. You see, as much as I truly wanted to commit suicide, a very tiny part of me didn't want to die without seeing Egypt; and I found that I couldn't 'allow' myself to travel there without first learning the impossible. What a predicament!

Naturally I have to admit that if push came to shove, Egypt would have been out the window and my hieroglyphic dictionaries in the bin, but I also cannot deny that my trying to learn this language played its small part in my recovery. It was something to focus on that took me one step closer to where I wanted to be, and it is often these little reminders of our true self that keep us believing life will be better one day.

Quick Tip

- There are always new things to learn even if you later decide that they are not quite your forte. The process itself is valuable, even if you perhaps don't achieve what was initially intended. Why not try and learn:

  - A language
  - A new skill
  - How to cook
  - To play an instrument
  - A sport
  - Some form of craft

- You might decide to teach yourself one or more of the above (or something entirely different) but do remember that there are courses available to help you along the way. These can be classes that you physically attend (see distraction number 91) but they could also be in the form of books, CD's or even material delivered online.

- Perhaps you could set yourself a target to learn something in a specific time frame. Having defined goals (see distraction number 62) is an excellent step towards being rid of your soul-destroyer, as it is a constant reminder that you have a purpose, and can help you to remember any achievements along the way.

Whatever you try and learn, remember that (as with many things) it can take time. Also, don't be put off if your first attempt doesn't go to plan. It might be that you simply need to switch methods or find a better-suited course. I was never very good at French when in school but I recently found that a CD-based course has helped me to rediscover the language. Sometimes learning can be about trial and error, and often the knowledge you leave with is that something you thought you wanted to learn; actually you didn't. It's all experience, and in my opinion, every experience is something we can learn from. Wait - Did we just fall into a never-ending loop?!

74 : CUT AWAY THE DEAD ENDS

Going to a salon is one of those things that is born out of a necessity but can be turned into a simple distraction. This is simply on the basis that it gets you out the house, and unless a disaster ensues; should have you on your way home enjoying a tiny boost to your confidence.

I'm sure you'll agree that there is something quite lovely about freshly cut hair. It feels manageable and smooth, and for some reason I find it much easier to rinse in the shower. Weirdly though, I don't seem to notice my hair getting in worse and worse condition over the weeks, so the great feeling after having it cut always comes as a tiny shock. How did I ever put up with it before? And exactly why is it that no matter what lotions and potions you use at home; you can never quite make your hair feel as nice as they do at the hairdressers?

Quick Tip

- Getting your hair cut doesn't have to be an idea just for the ladies! Split ends affect us all, and most of us can always do with a bit of extra pampering. Book yourself an appointment at your local, or favourite hair salon and try and allow yourself to look forward to and enjoy it. The person cutting your hair won't mind if you barely speak, but if you can leave those negative thoughts at the door; your mind will probably appreciate an hour of friendly banter.

- If you'd feel more comfortable then ask a friend to accompany you. I have days when I crave company for simple things, and others where I feel completely fine and able to cope on my own. It is what friends are for. It might also be worth trying to figure out a rough idea of the kind of style that you'd like, so do have a look at some pictures beforehand.

- You don't have to spend loads of money just to feel good. If you've picked somewhere that you'd like to make an appointment, remember to ask about any special offers or discounts that could be running. Perhaps you could ask for an appointment with one of the junior stylists? Another option is to find a hairdresser who will come to your home. I've always loved the idea of this; especially now that I feel increasingly old amongst the young and trendy people working in our local salon.

- I personally wouldn't recommend opting for anything too drastic. As much as it might seem cool now to shave your head and dye your eyebrows pink, it is often extremely difficult to filter out genuinely good ideas from those which are spawn from depression. Don't risk it!

In my experience with mental illness, I never even felt worthy of the air I breathed, never mind spending time and money to forge my appearance. What I was denying myself however, was the opportunity to discover little boosts in my confidence - such as actually liking a new hairstyle or difference in the way I looked. I believe that it is important for you to allow yourself this chance, because much of combating depression is discovering the elements in yourself and your life that you do like; and changing those that you don't.

75 : PACK A PICNIC

I am a firm believer that food is not just about sustaining us in our busy lives - It is here to be thoroughly enjoyed. Our lifestyles often mean that we are forced to buy food whilst out and about, yet it can be so much more rewarding when you plan a little bit in advance and take a picnic.

When I'm feeling hungry enough to eat my own hand, I find that seeing someone else tuck into their glorious picnic of fresh food; made just the way they like it, always yields the response 'I wish I'd thought of that.'

The great thing about picnics is that they help us to feel self-sustained. We don't 'need' that greasy burger van or expensive sandwich if we are armed with a cooler full of newly-baked bread, cheese, juice, and homemade cookies. Of course this does take organisational skills, but it is the very act of toning our ability to prepare, which builds our strong foundations to steady us during rough seas.

Quick Tip

- Combine this distraction with any of the ones that get you outside exploring and you have the beginnings of a great day out. If you know you are going to be away from home during lunch, take a picnic with you. We've seen families eating their homemade sandwiches in the car park to a National Trust house and they still made me feel jealous. Just being outside with nice food is enough to take my thoughts away from that familiar negative path; even if the surroundings are not quite a postcard photo. We all know how much attractions charge for even a basic sandwich, so you'll also be saving money. Why fork out for bland cheese and stale bread, when you can be munching on your favourite ciabatta with that extra dollop of sour cream.

- You don't need to already have plans to go out to enjoy this distraction. Why not simply grab some food from your house and go and have a picnic in your garden or local park? If it's too rainy or miserable to be outside, why not have one indoors? It might sound silly, but with a picnic in your front room you can pretend you are anywhere in the world. Make-believe shouldn't just be confined to the youngsters. Lay out the picnic blanket and imagine you are somewhere else.

FREE

76 : SEE YOUR FRIENDS

I truly believe that society is forcing us to become less and less 'connected' with others, despite the communication channels being more open than ever. Isolation fosters depression, and humouring our solitary impulses often puts us in danger of being consumed by misery.

In my opinion, 'liking' something on 'Facebook', or making a quick comment online to let someone know you are there, isn't enough; especially for those of us who 'see' the negative in everything. It's a dangerous game and I genuinely think that we would all benefit from going back to seeing our friends the old fashioned way.

Now is probably the perfect time to log-off your computer, and instead, arrange some trips out with the people you care about. The cinema, the pub; anything really. It might help you appreciate that friends really do like you, and are there to offer support (not just in a virtual world). In turn, this might help you to start liking yourself a little.

Again, just getting out of the house can give your mind the tiny bit of breathing space that it needs, even more so if some of your problems are centered around the place you call home.

Try to not rely too heavily on the Internet to keep in touch with your friends. Nothing can beat face-to-face contact, yet in a somewhat sad fashion, the modern age is almost phasing this out. Picking up the phone and speaking to your friends can be so much easier than writing them a message and hoping that they aren't too swamped down in cyberspace to read it and reply.

If you have ever felt the frustration of posting something online, only to find that no one has time to reply, then you will understand when I say that deep friendship links tend to be created by 'real' interaction.

Quick Tip

- Give yourself a break from social networking sites and make time to see your friends. It doesn't matter if you simply meet up at home and chat the night away over a glass of wine or endless cups of tea. True friends don't need an exciting plan in order to meet up; they will be happy just to be in your company.

- If you feel as though you need to take the pressure off conversation, then arrange to do something with your friend, which commands less talking. The cinema or theatre can be great for this, as can sporty activities such as go-karting, climbing or swimming. Even having someone else to exercise with can give you the inspiration to start in the first place, and we already know that physical exertion is one of the keys to fighting those negative feelings.

- Whenever your friends ask you to come out with them, try and accept the invitation; even if there is a little voice in your head telling you that you don't feel like it. I found that this voice tended to speak the words of depression, and when I ignored it and went out anyway, it usually left me feeling much better in myself.

77 : COLOUR YOUR LIFE

As each year passes and another hair turns grey, more and more I have realised that my home environment is especially important to my wellbeing. Whether living with family, renting a flat, house or bedsit, or paying a mortgage towards a place of your own, it is important that you actually enjoy going home.

When I started noticing that I didn't really like the colours our home was painted, room-by-room I started re-decorating. It was time-consuming and exhausting, but it gave me a great project to be distracted with and I found it extremely therapeutic.

Something such as painting can be very rewarding because you can actually see the progress with each stroke of the brush (or roller). Suddenly, colours that I loved surrounded me and I felt satisfied for having been the one to put them there. On days when I woke up feeling a bit fed up, I would find pleasure just from sitting in our sky-blue bathroom and admiring the finished product.

Personally, I find something as simple as colour in my home can help remind me that the world isn't the black and grey that depression makes me believe it is.

Quick Tip

- You don't have to be artistic to decide to re-decorate. Have a look through house and home magazines for inspiration, or even just check out the colour swatch brochures available at DIY stores. Think about what would complement the furniture you will put in each space. If the room doesn't get much natural light, don't pick colours that are too dark. We opted for just one coloured wall in a room that barely sees the sun. You can have great fun just planning the change, even if you decide to get someone else to do the painting for you.

78 : GIVE A GOOD GIFT

We all live in a very materialistic society, yet physical things cannot always bring us true happiness. Sometimes the joy that an object brings may be very short-lived and could leave us feeling rather deflated. However, the nice feeling from giving a good gift can last so much longer, and is naturally a more selfless act.

Quick Tip

Next time you find yourself pondering over the choice of Christmas gift or birthday present, why not give the following a thought: -

- Instead of buying another DVD or set of toiletries, why not sponsor a child, animal or tree in the recipient's name.

- Perhaps you could buy them an ethical 'good gift' - such as a goat for a family in Africa, or warm hats for the elderly. You could see if your local charity shop has these kinds of gifts on offer, or they can easily be bought online. (Don't worry; you won't have to squeeze a real goat into the post-box.) Usually there is also a great choice of cheaper gifts available, which would make great stocking fillers.

- Try and buy fair-trade gifts so that you can rest tight knowing that someone else isn't paying the price for our convenience.

- There are other things that you could do which should help you to create that warm, fuzzy feeling inside from knowing you have given a little bit of good back to the world. How about setting up a regular payment to charity, or filling out organ donation card. Many of us forget how lucky we are in the part of the world we live, but it is never too late to help others.

Knowing that you have spent your money on things that won't end up under the bed collecting dust can be quite refreshing; even if the person you give this gift to doesn't perhaps fully appreciate it. The important thing here in terms of being a good distraction, is that it can help you to feel valued and caring.

These are the kinds of emotions than anchor us, and when depression tries to make us feel worthless; we have something to fight back with. I truly believe that much of recovery is about finding that sense of self-worth, and it is understandable that this will not simply come from physical objects around us.

FREE TO

79 : DANCE THE NIGHT AWAY

I would never have pegged myself for a dancer - ever. I wasn't the sort of person to go clubbing (in fact I have never been to one in my life) and the thought of going to a class terrified me. Whilst my friends arranged nights out, I would happily settle myself on the sofa with a DVD and cup of tea.

As I grew older and less self-loathing, my hips grew outwards and I realised that it was time to turn my newfound confidence into some form of energetic movement; before I ended up needing to replace my entire wardrobe.

I signed up to a gym near work and like most people, I was enthusiastic at first until winter set in and then I hardly ever went; telling myself it was too cold to go out.

On the day I inquired about cancelling my membership, the member of staff politely asked me if I'd ever tried any of the classes on offer. He talked about how popular the Zumba class was; explaining it was a mixture of various Latin dance.

Feeling guilty about cancelling so soon, the following Monday I clung to the back wall of the class with the other newbies, secretly enjoying every exhausting minute of it. I went home feeling healthy, sexy and energised, and the depression I felt about my weight was nowhere to be seen.

Dancing had given me more than I anticipated, and it quickly became an excellent distraction from depression, laziness and fast food.

Quick Tip

- If the thought of joining a gym sends you running to the freezer for comforting chips and easy pizza, don't cross dance off the list just yet. Why not look for a specific dance class close to home; which you can pay for as and when you feel up to it. If the class isn't right for you, try another. A different teacher can get you from loathing to loving their class.

- If you still aren't convinced about dancing in public, how about buying a dance fitness DVD so you can work out in your living room without having to worry about feeling embarrassed or unfit. The beauty of this is that you can work completely at your own pace and only when you feel like it. I've often found myself deciding to work on my Salsa late at night whilst everyone else is out. Having a DVD to dance to meant I could distract myself even at the most inconvenient of times; which was usually how depression fitted into my life.

FREE

80 : DIG FOR YOUR ROOTS

When I was at my most depressed it felt as though I was the black sheep of the family; that no-one understood what I was experiencing. I felt alone. Almost all of my mum's side of the family lived abroad and I barely knew any of my relatives. This lack of belonging only heightened these feelings; although I was totally unaware of the effect it was having on me at the time.

It wasn't until I made the unusual decision to travel to Florida with my mum to attend a cousin's wedding - a cousin I had never met, that I started to see the benefit of having family. These people were interesting, caring and understanding. I found myself eager to learn about my roots and fascinated to hear that some of them had even felt the way I did. Suddenly I didn't feel so alone and my paranoia's about being 'different' started to fade away.

Quick Tip

- Get a pen and paper out and draw your family tree. Are there relatives you don't know much about? Can anyone in your family fill in some of the blanks? Perhaps you can search for people online? Think how much you know about each of these individuals. Do you ever wonder if someone in your family has shared similar feelings or experiences to those you are going through now? Maybe it is time to get to know your family more. Why not arrange a reunion or try to get in contact with certain people. Learning about your family's past can be interesting and exciting, even if it does mean doing some digging.

Sophia Gill

FREE

81 : EMBRACE CHRISTMAS

Christmas can be an extremely difficult time for anyone who is already feeling even a little bit rubbish, because it has the power to magnify those negative feelings and render us useless.

Thrust upon us as a time for family, loved ones, and new beginnings, Christmas and New Year are more often a time for overwhelming loneliness and fear. 'Tis only the season to be jolly if you are lucky enough to not be terrified of it!

Personally, I used to find those months at the end of the year to be the worst of them all. They are grey, cold, rainy, and uninspiring, and I always struggled to look forward to the Christmas holidays. Seeing and hearing about everyone else's plans for their big family reunions only made me wonder why it wasn't the same in ours, and I would hate the inevitable arguments that sprung up about who is going to see who on what day and for how long.

The reality is, a rather large number of people also feel the same way about Christmas, and it is not the most looked-forward to holiday as we are led to believe. I used to feel worse because I plagued myself with thoughts of what a wonderful time everyone else was having, and yet here I was waiting for it to all be over already. The thing is, you really should stop torturing yourself with thoughts about how fantastic other peoples Christmas' are and focus on making your own one better - or at very least, bearable.

As soon as I stopped letting Christmas and New Year be this great pressure on me to be happy no matter what, suddenly I didn't mind them as much. In fact, now I'm even starting to wish they would come around sooner.

Quick Tip

- This festive season, do whatever it takes to make yourself look forward to it. If you already do, then why not share your enthusiasm with someone who needs it.

- If you would rather plan something, which might mean you will be away from home for the Christmas period, don't let yourself succumb to the pressure of others. You have to do what feels right for you. If that means missing out on your mum's turkey dinner, it still doesn't mean this is not the right decision. Take the time to talk about your plans with the people concerned - you might even find that they embrace the idea too. We all feel this invisible pressure to spend Christmas in a certain way, but in reality, it *is* just another day. New Year is the same. How you choose to spend them is up to you. I was just as happy celebrating in Vegas for New Year than I was the year I fell asleep before midnight on the sofa watching 'The Polar Express'. Don't feel as though you have to stick to a certain routine.

- Check local newspapers or have a look online for any ice rinks that might be popping up nearby. A leisurely skate on a cool, dark winter's night outside a classic landmark might be just what you need to get you in the Christmas spirit. Ask your friends, colleagues and family if they are interested in joining you; you could even make it into a group event or staff party. If you're not much of a skater, perhaps there is a Christmas fair or show that you could arrange to see? I often find that the more I try to resist Christmas; the unhappier I am about it. Try embracing the season instead!

- Arm yourself with a good selection of films, a fluffy blanket and a soothing cup of tea or hot chocolate; ready to pass away the evening when the weather outside is blistery and depressing.

- If the weather doesn't affect you, make the effort to continue outdoor activities even when most people would say it is too cold or wet to do so. You might even find that you enjoy it more with everyone else tucked up at home.

- To help with the pressure of Christmas shopping, buy things as and when you see them. Don't feel as though you have to wait until December. In fact if you start much earlier, you'll be more likely to think carefully about each purchase and make the most of special offers. This way the cost is spread much further out too, so you won't need to sell a Kidney a week before Christmas, just to be able to afford it.

- As adults, often what is missing from our Christmas is the way in which children see it. Sometimes, every year that passes is just another reminder that we no longer feel the same way about Christmas as we used to. Children can be that missing element and whilst there isn't exactly a quick fix for this, perhaps you can focus on a niece or nephew this year, and add to or make them a Christmas stocking. If your family is already grown up now, why not look at doing something to help a stranger? This Christmas I'm filling shoeboxes with presents to give to a charity, which then sends them to underprivileged children all over the world.

Sophia Gill

82 : THESE CREATURES CAN BITE

Whether you are a big fan of animals or not, going to a zoo or aquarium can be a wonderful distraction because - like us, animals are totally unpredictable. This is great for times when you need to take your mind off negative things as it means you are kept on your toes; waiting to see what will happen next.

Whilst it is unlikely that something extraordinary is going to occur while you are at the zoo; I very much doubt a lion will escape and chase you down the street, it can be very calming to simply sit quietly and watch the animals carry on their business.

I had time alone in Birmingham to kill just after I had some bad news that I didn't get the job I so desperately needed. I was struggling to not let this disappointment thoroughly depress me and recognised that I needed a good distraction to drag me away from those downward spiralling thoughts.

Instead of walking around the shops being sad that I had no money to spend, I decided to visit the aquarium. I'm not much of a sea life fan, yet I felt extremely at peace sat on the ledge at the side of the stingray tank; watching the creatures swim around and around. The ambient light was just enough to keep the smallish room feel cosy and warm, and the lack of people on this mid-week afternoon helped me feel as though there was no pressure of time.

Of course there might not be any true escape from the thoughts that we have, but often a change of scenery can be enough to deflect them. In terms of self-harm, postponing that cut even just for a moment is definitely a move in the right direction. It might be that we need to not self-harm for just long enough until we can get help, or it might be a case of needing to know that by not cutting, we ARE in control. Either way, this is the very reason for every distraction, and finding out which ones work for you.

Quick Tip

- If you've not been to the zoo since a school trip many years ago, it's time to remind yourself how interesting they are. Zoo's combine unpredictable animal behaviour with some fresh air and a good walk around outside. If you are short in time; just go and see your favourite animals, or if it doesn't matter how long it takes; go and see them all. There are certain enclosures that you might normally walk past; but this time, why not give them a glance.

- Aquariums can also make for great days out and can more often be found closer to city centres. Don't make the same mistake I did by buying a prawn sandwich before I got there. Lunch didn't feel so right after a day spent admiring the live ones!

- Often there are vouchers for discounted entry to places like these. Keep an eye in newspapers and supermarket leaflets, or check for offers online.

- Don't forget, just because they might be targeted at families and schools, zoos and aquariums are great places for people of all ages. However, if you do know you'd never find the energy to go alone, see if a friend or family member would like to join you. If you know anyone with children, they might even jump at the chance to take their kids along too.

FREE TO

83 : EXPERIENCE HISTORY

To take a quote from the philosopher George Santayana, 'Those who cannot remember the past are condemned to repeat it.' History can be shocking, fascinating, inspiring and unbelievable; which are many of the ideal ingredients for a great distraction.

After a fairly nasty accident, which caused my beloved car to be written off and my doctor to sign me off from work with whiplash and stress, depression crept silently back into my life and begged me to self-harm again. With no work to keep me from this destructive path, it was all too easy to slip back into old habits.

It was a spur of the moment decision to visit the Science museum in London: because I was in the area anyway to see a doctor about my insurance claim, which led me to discover how therapeutic museums can be.

Walking around the museum with my iPod playing quietly on shuffle, it was great to re-visit a place that I hadn't been to since I was a child. I began remembering things from my school years that I thought were long forgotten, and ended up on the train feeling just a tiny bit smarter.

Learning is such an important part of all aspects of life that it naturally has its own chapter in this book. But just as the quote says, a big part of learning is to ensure we don't keep repeating the same mistakes. Museums are there to remind us the work our ancestors have done; to inspire and teach us; and help us lead fulfilling lives. As a bonus however, a museum can offer us a moment of peace during a time when our lives feel chaotic.

Quick Tip

- Many of us carry on our busy lives without even looking twice at a museum. Often it is only for children, or as tourists that we take the time to visit them, yet they are wonderful places for all of us. Make a list of the ones you've been meaning to see and start acting on it. I was fascinated with Egyptian history for many years before it even dawned on me to go to the British museum.

- If you are the sort of person who finds it helpful to see how people have historically coped with much worse situations than you find yourself in, how about making a trip to a war museum? Personally I find that thinking about how worse things could be only makes me feel guilty for my depression, however I appreciate that not everyone reacts in this way.

- If a better distraction for you would be something that won't stir up as many emotions, why not visit something like a science museum or art gallery?

- Perhaps there is a temporary exhibition that will be in your area soon? Have a search online to see what's going on near you. I travelled to many different places to see Titanic exhibitions, and each one was just as fascinating as the last.

- Is there something in particular that interests you such as the Aztecs, ancient Egyptians or Romans? Artefacts can be scattered all over various museums so it is worth visiting different places to find out what they have.

FREE TO 🐷🐷🐷

84 : FIX IT

Has the shed door fallen off or the fence panel collapsed? Does that shelf need putting up or the wonky table need fixing? There has never been a better time to finally get around to those DIY jobs that you keep putting off.

It doesn't matter if you own your own property or are renting from a landlord or council, I'm almost certain that there is at least one DIY job out there.

Our shed needed new hinges for years, yet there never seemed to be a good opportunity to do it. Determined to take my own advice, I came home from a depressing day at work and went straight out into the garden. It might have been unusual timing I admit; working away in the dark on a drizzly evening, whilst my stomach rumbled for dinner, however I did find myself feeling extremely proud afterwards.

The great thing about DIY is that the satisfaction from having actually fixed something yourself; whether it was challenging or not, is not a feeling you can easily replicate. Not only that, but there are practical benefits as well. Just think how great it will be when you don't have to prop up that wonky table at dinnertime, or stack things on the floor because the shelf isn't up yet.

If you make that decision to distract yourself with the odd job around the house, this can also stop those thoughts such as 'I must get round to doing that'. Thinking things like this are negative because they act as little pressures on you, and whilst ordinarily a bit of pressure can be great, depression has a habit of turning normal things into nightmares. Chances are you are battling enough negativity already and so even getting rid of one such thought is going to be a bonus.

Literally being able to see the difference you have made in your home is a great boost to your self-esteem; and this is bound to be playing a major part in why you needed a distraction in the first place. Anything that forces you to appreciate yourself, your skills, and your life even a tiny bit more, is a massive step in the right direction.

Quick Tip

- Have a walk around your home and make a mental note of what needs doing. Write a list if you think that will help. You'd be surprised just how many of those little jobs are still waiting for you. We are yet to re-do a kitchen shelf with a bit of a slant and I'm sure there are loads of other odd jobs I could distract myself with if needed.

- If you can't complete these jobs because you are missing something, borrow the tools, get yourself down to the nearest DIY shop, or order the items online. Even if they sit there unused for a while, at least next time you need this distraction you will be completely ready for it.

- If a job is looking far too big for just you alone, why not ask family and friends to pitch in. You might find someone you know has done the exact same thing in their home and has loads of advice on making it easier for you.

Ladies - don't pass up on this distraction because you assume it's one for the men. There are DIY jobs that can just as easily be done by the fairest of the sexes, and perhaps we might even do it better! I did a lot of the DIY in our house before I met my fiancé, and even now he's less familiar with the drill than I am. Sometimes it just takes one job to give you the confidence to tackle the next, and this applies whether you are man or woman.

Caution

Be careful. Don't attempt something that you aren't sure about - some things should really be left to the professionals. You don't want to drill a hole in the wall to end up knee high in a burst water main. Get advice if you need to, and above all; stay safe.

Sophia Gill

FREE

85 : GET SPONSORED

One of the most distressing things that anyone could say to me when I was at my worst with depression, is 'just think about all those dying people in the world.' If it wasn't bad enough that I couldn't explain or understand the reasons for feeling the way I did, people accidently made me feel guilty for just being me. This was not the right time for being rational. I was not going to 'snap out' of my depressed state by being reminded of the atrocities of the world, however I did later learn that there was something I could do to help. This distraction helped both me and others.

We all have things that we would find challenging and often these challenges can become sponsored events. Asides from eating my dinner out of a cat bowl on the floor when I was thirteen to raise money for 'Comic relief', as an adult my first real sponsored challenge was an abseil off the top of a tower block at work.

I found that having set goals: to raise a certain amount of money and also conquer my fear of heights (if only for that half an hour), gave me a great distraction from the melancholy that so often crept into work with me. I felt such a sense of achievement and reward from that one event that I also signed up for a sponsored skydive and shark-dive (and came out from both with stories to tell).

There are so many worthwhile causes out there and so many ways we can raise money to support them, that with a bit of thought I am sure you can find something that suits you.

Quick Tip

- Is there a charity in particular that you would like to support? Maybe you or someone close to you has recently needed the help of a particular charity, hospital or group. Why not ask if they need help fundraising.

- Have a think about what type of event you'd like to take part in. It could be a sponsored walk, run, swim or day of silence.

- If there isn't already an event that suits you, make one up. You are 'allowed' to be sponsored for anything remember. As long as you can explain to your sponsors why that particular thing is a challenge for you, then I'm sure people will be happy to support you.

- If adrenaline is more your thing, how about a skydive, climb, or bungee jump? If you can't find an organised event that fits with your schedule, why not organise one yourself?

Remember it's not about setting goals so high that you struggle to reach them. Set yourself a challenge that you know you can achieve with a bit of effort.

FREE (AT HOME)

TO 🐷 🐷 (IF YOU BUY ROUNDS)

86 : QUENCH YOUR THIRST

I have to admit now - this is one distraction that I have only really half done, and that is because I don't drink alcohol. To me, the idea of 'going for a drink' means a cold glass of lemonade with a slice of lemon.

I avoided the lure of alcohol at the age when I was legally allowed to start drinking because I was already battling one addiction: self-harm. I hardly needed another one! As I fought on, not drinking started to make more and more sense, until it became completely normal.

Choosing to become the dedicated driver made sense in my life. I had come far enough along my road to recovery to know to avoid things that may hinder progress. However, I appreciate that everyone treats alcohol differently, and for some it can make a great distraction.

Going for a drink with your friends might be that great excuse for you to get out of the house for an evening and enjoy spending time other people. Or drinking at home could be all you need to take the edge off, so that you relax and calm down. Whichever one suits you the most, use this time to quench your thirst - in moderation!

Quick Tip

- Is there a nice cool beer in the fridge, or bottle of wine that you've been saving? Even a lemonade or fruit juice can suit the moment. Sit down, relax, and enjoy the flavours.

- Go and meet your friends in the pub or bar - even if you don't fancy a drinking night. You might enjoy it more than you thought. (See distraction number 76.)

- If you'd rather give yourself more of a purpose with this distraction, how about trying something like wine tasting? You could go on a specific course, or perhaps teach yourself about all the different varieties. Mike started doing this when he realised that he would quite like to know more about the drinks he was choosing when we ate out. His self-taught course has been a great way to spend the evening, and his newfound knowledge has made wine shopping much more fun.

Caution

Don't turn to alcohol if you know it's going to have terrible consequences. I have always been teetotal because deep down I know that with the depression and self-harm, I would more than likely end up an alcoholic. I just have an addictive personality and didn't want to add to my troubles. This idea is only in here because I know not everyone treats drinking the same, and for some it can be an excellent distraction. However, if you know that it will be more of a hindrance than help, skip this chapter and pick another distraction.

87 : PUT ON A PLAY

The thought of acting may make you cringe in fear, but putting on some form of play can be an excellent way to ignore the voices of depression and concentrate instead on something make-believe.

In my younger years, a friend and I used to spend much of our summer holidays turning books into scripts so that we could act out the story to our parents and siblings. We would spend days doing drawings to hang up in a pretend gallery, and then charge our mums 20p to effectively walk upstairs 'through the gallery' to view our 'show'.

Focusing on something like this when you are battling depression works because it gives you that opportunity to step outside your own skin. If even for a moment, taking on the role of a character in a play gives you breathing space from those worsening thoughts, and this is vital in your recovery.

Quick Tip

- Perhaps you could join a drama group and work with others to perform a small-scale production. This is an excellent opportunity to meet new people; which can also help to free you from the rut. Joining something like this can improve your self-confidence whilst also provide you with a better sense of community. Often our lives are lacking those links to other people, and depression loves to feed off this sense of isolation.

- If you haven't got the confidence to perform in front of people, why not create a puppet show for the children in your family? Perhaps you can work on something to entertain them at the next family gathering - maybe on Christmas day whilst everyone is recovering from lunch. The great thing about puppets is that you are hidden from view, and this makes it much easier to combat shyness.

- Once you've mastered some circus skills from distraction number 93 or magic tricks from distraction number 92, why not share the fun by performing them in front of friends and family. You don't need a huge audience; even just showing one friend could help you to feel that sense of achievement. The fun that comes with it is simply a bonus.

FREE TO

88 : A DAY AT THE RACES

When I ask Mike what he fancies doing this weekend, he might suggest going to a National Trust house or watching a movie, but I don't think I will ever hear him say 'let's go to the races.' For us it's just one of those more unusual things to do, yet it can actually make for a great evening away from negative thoughts.

Depression would have us fester at home stewing in anger and hurt if it had the choice; and this is exactly why you should do the opposite. Getting out - even when our minds tell us that we would rather eat glass, is always worth it because at very least it is a change. Just as depression feels timeless, it also creates a sensation that our lives are on a permanent repeat. Breaking away from this monotony is the healthy choice because it forms our weapon against this stagnant illness.

Quick Tip

- There are many different types of races that you can go to watch. How about taking yourself along to see a: -

  o   Horse race.
  o   Dog race.
  o   Car race - real or remote-controlled.
  o   Regatta.
  o   Sporting event, such as a marathon.

215

- Perhaps you can use one of these suggestions as an excuse to dress up in fancy clothes and treat yourself to a bit of luxury. Why not book the more exclusive box tickets and spoil yourself with champagne and strawberries in half time. You could even combine this with distraction number 75, and take along some of your favourite foods to savour while you watch. It might sound like too much effort initially, but I often find that I am very grateful for having bothered - especially when I am sipping tea as everyone else admires from afar.

- You might find that some of these ideas inspire you to participate in racing events, and this is also a wonderful distraction. Having a goal such as training to win a particular race keeps us focussed on something positive, and often the negatives simply don't have the time to seep in.

Remember that going to watch a race is not all about placing bets. It is perfectly fine to simply go for the atmosphere - you don't have to blow money in the process. If you do decide to have a flutter, set yourself a limit beforehand and do everything in your power to stick to it. If you know that you find it difficult to resist temptation, how about leaving any credit cards at home and only taking a certain amount of cash with you. Put someone else in charge of 'an emergency card' if you'd feel safer knowing there was a back-up plan for getting home.

89 : GROW YOUR OWN

Although this idea has many crossovers with distraction numbers 64 and 96, it is definitely worthy of its own chapter.

Growing your own fruit, herbs and/or vegetables is never nearly as difficult as it sounds, and is so much more rewarding than buying from the shops. With supermarkets taking the place of the high-street greengrocer and society pushing for organic produce, there has never been a better time to turn to your own back garden for a healthy snack or dinner.

There are a number of reasons why I recommend giving this distraction a go, but the most simple is that growing your own is cost-effective. If you are organised enough to plant from seed then the savings are maximised, but even if you buy an already established plant; it wont take long before you have eaten your money's worth in fresh ingredients.

More important than money however, is the satisfaction guarantee. Just as watching any seed sprout for the first time can help you feel that you've done something worthwhile by planting it, with this you will literally be able to eat the fruits of your labour. Home-grown fruits and vegetables somehow always taste nicer than bought ones and are obviously much more fresh and organic. Naturally you will only be able to plant those suitable for your environment, so don't get your heart set on growing pineapples if you live in Bromley!

This is the kind of distraction that may mean you just plant a couple of tomatoes in your windowsill box which you keep for a few months, or you could enjoy so much that you eventually dedicate a large portion of your garden to it year after year. Either way, it is certainly worth giving it a go.

Having plants to care for on a daily basis can break us out of that depressive routine that we so often find ourselves in, and can have a real positive impact on our mood. Although I must admit that I'm already a big fan of great food, I truly enjoy picking the ripe tomatoes off the scraggly plants next to our wonky shed; ready for our supper.

I find that growing our own also makes me want to eat more healthily; possibly because I wouldn't want to feel like I'd wasted the effort I put in, and because I truly hate throwing away food. Eating better is naturally a very good step towards becoming more positive anyway and so this distraction is one that can really stick around for the long haul.

Quick Tip

- Tomato plants are pretty easy to grow and can be put in a container if you are short of space. My mum has two boxes on the windowsill of her flat with baby tomato plants in and they do very well. Herbs are another easy one; again taking up very little space.

- Browse your local garden centre and see which seeds would be perfect to plant at this time of year. Also check the kind of soil and light they need and make sure they are suitable for your home.

- Perhaps you know someone who is already growing their own produce and would be happy to give you a cutting or some seeds from their crops. Speak to family and friends for help and advice.

- If your windowsills are already full but you'd love to be in charge of your own little vegetable plot, why not look at renting one? Often there is a bit of a wait for one with the local council, but you can always register to be put on the waiting list. Or maybe someone you know has a garden they wouldn't mind some help with. Often once you start growing fruits and vegetables the plants produce more than enough to share. You might even find that this becomes a project that you embark on together.

- If you'd rather use this distraction as a once only kind of thing, how about planting a fruit tree? They take very little maintenance but remember that not all trees will stay small for long. Make sure you check to see how big the tree will likely grow. A few years ago we planted a small apple tree in our very little garden, and digging the hole deep enough for it was an excellent way to be rid of the anger I was feeling at the time. I've barely had to pay any more attention to it since, and every time I look out the kitchen window at it a smile creeps across my face.

Sophia Gill

FREE (IF YOU HAVE AN INSTRUMENT)

TO

90 : HIT THE NOTE

In one short and sweet sentence: learn to play an instrument.

As already mentioned in distraction number 9, music can be an extremely powerful tool. Whilst I used to believe it was only certain people who were blessed with the natural ability to play an instrument, I later learned that some instruments are suited to us less musically talented souls. Learning to play an instrument might still be a big challenge, especially if you have your heart set on one of the more difficult ones, but don't let age or experience put you off.

Being rather fickle with my hobbies and interests, over time I have naturally collected myself enough instruments to create a small one-man band. Ok, so I might not have used them as much as I hoped, but they each served a purpose at one point in time. I still love them all dearly without regretting their purchase and would struggle to get rid of any of them now.

For me, learning to play an instrument was an excellent distraction whereby hours would pass without my even noticing. The Djembe (African drum) was excellent for beating out those aggressive tendencies and was the perfect instrument of choice during my self-harming years. The guitar fitted into my life when I began to mellow out and appreciate the concentration that playing cords needed, whilst the violin was fun to learn when I had Mike there to giggle with me - as I produced a sequence of strangled cat sounds.

Quick Tip

- If you already own an instrument (or two), now is the time to dig it out, dust it off, and get practising. Why not invest in a book to help you learn to play, or perhaps have a look online for some helpful videos, tabs, sheet music or tips.

- If you've never given music a go, head down to a local music shop and have a chat about which instruments are good for beginners. You don't need to be able to read sheet music and some instruments are perfect for the occasional dabble. If you can't afford to buy the instrument of your choice, perhaps there is a rental scheme available or a cheaper version you can pick up second hand. Maybe a friend or relative has something you can borrow instead?

- Is there a particular song that inspires you to play, or a style of music that you wish you knew more about? My decision to learn the violin was born purely out of my fascination with Cirque Du Soleil, and wanting to learn a particular song helped me stay focussed and passionate. Although you can't run before you can walk; having a goal in mind is helpful, as long as you stay realistic and don't let yourself become too disheartened if things progress slowly.

- If you would rather not teach yourself, have a look to see if anyone in your area gives lessons or if there are any classes that you can join. There might even be some amateur bands that you can practice with if you are at the right level.

- Naturally the more you practise the better you will become, but don't be put off by the thought that you have to give this distraction some serious time; it is fine if you only want to play every now and then. You won't be able to join the Royal Philharmonic Orchestra, but instruments can be fun without attaining professional levels.

- Learning to play an instrument can give you a major confidence boost, especially when you hit the right notes. Not only is it something that you can do with complete independence, it can also be a very social pastime. The right kind of music is extremely soothing and this feeling is heightened when you are actually playing it yourself. Not many distractions can tick all of those boxes and so this has got to be one that comes highly recommended. This, from someone who feared music lessons at school and can't play for toffee; means a lot!

Sophia Gill

91 : GO TO CLASS

I have always really struggled to find the enthusiasm to drag my lazy arse to a class, especially when it's cold and miserable outside. My initial thought is always that I'd rather wallow around at home, yet I have never actually regretted those times when I do make it out.

Out of the many that I have tried, lunchtime Pilates classes at work are the ones I most frequently stick to. It's possibly because I have to take my break and eat lunch at a certain time and once that happens I feel committed. I may drag myself there wishing I'd found an excuse, but I always leave feeling so pleased that I didn't. It's the same every week and I still don't understand why I carry this negativity. I guess it's just in my nature.

However, what I have learned is that often depression can make us feel like we've achieved nothing. When we fight these thoughts away with qualifications and purpose, depression struggles to keep its grip. My Pilates classes help me to feel as though I am achieving my goal to tone up, and other classes in the past have reminded me that I do have interests and skills. It is introducing these small bouts of positive feeling that beating depression is all about.

There are always so many classes to choose from that there is bound to be something that takes your fancy. It doesn't matter if you simply go once and decide it's not for you. It is better to go and discover something new, than to not go at all.

Quick Tip

- Try and find out if there are any classes that interest you in the local area. Remember that they could be classes you attend after work, in your lunch-break, or even at the weekend. If you need some ideas, how about trying one or more of the following: -

  o An exercise class such as Yoga, Pilates, swimming or dancing.
  o A class to learn a language or qualification.
  o Perhaps one to brush up on existing skills, or take those qualifications to the next level.

- If you can't find anything to suit you, perhaps there is an online class that you can subscribe to. I've completed my whole degree online with the Open University and it has been far more convenient for me than going to a physical University. You may find it more challenging, but usually the best reward comes from things that we find the hardest.

FREE TO

92 : IT'S MAGIC

I've recently noticed that it was around the same time that I was fighting my biggest battle with depression that the box of magic tricks under my bed grew at an alarming rate. The funniest thing was, I wasn't even that into magic. My best friend at the time was keen and I was definitely influenced by his fascination, but as much as I did love to see a good magician at work, I certainly wasn't looking for a career change.

More than anything, I started trying to learn how to do tricks purely because my logical mind never stopped asking how things were done. The magic tricks that my friend and I saw in shows used to puzzle me and I yearned to unlock the secret.

What I did learn along the way was that magic is an excellent distraction and allows you to be as involved as you can find the energy for. There are simple tricks; which are merely down to clever equipment - the type of deck of cards, or a cleverly constructed box, but there are also tricks that demand excruciatingly complex skill and practice.

Learning a magic trick can simply be something you distract yourself with for five minutes, or a hobby that you turn to time and time again for hours on end. There will always be someone interested in watching you perform magic - even if it means videoing yourself so you can upload the tricks onto the Internet for feedback. I once took my favourite magic trick to a theme park with me and used it to pass the time whilst queuing for a ride. People might have thought I was either nuts or employed by the park, but the whole experience gave me a great boost in confidence; especially when the trick worked.

Quick Tip

- If you already own some magic tricks (and I'm not talking about the Marvin's magic set you had as a kid here) dig them out and get practicing. Just think; it might shock your family when you levitate by the tree after scoffing down Christmas dinner, but it will certainly get the conversation rolling.

- If magic is something you've never tried before, remember you are never too old to give it a go. It isn't just children who are impressed with skilful magicians and you don't need Vegas style stages or lights to make good magic work.

- Not all of us have magic shops on the high street (unless you live in Blackpool perhaps) but you can easily buy tricks on the Internet. Check out specialist online retailers or see if you can find a bargain on ebay. It might be an idea to set yourself a spending limit, as the better tricks can quickly get expensive.

- Try and build up a nice variety of magic tricks to try out - ranging from easy to hard, ones that involve a participant to ones that you can do on your own, and tricks that require skill to ones that are totally dependent on a clever piece of equipment. I was never too good at card ones: I found sleight of hand too difficult with my small hands. Instead I preferred brass tricks, which had a nice quality feel to them and felt like money well spent.

Some tricks might sound amazing by the description, but do bear in mind that they might be disappointing once you know how it's done; you'll quickly learn to spot the good ones. My personal favourites were a skewer through the tongue trick, which was so bad I was ashamed to even show my friend the 'magic' skewer, and a precision engineered special pound coin costing £30, which we deduced he must have actually spent by accident!

FREE TO

93 : JOIN THE CIRCUS

The title got your attention there didn't it! Although I don't actually mean you should quit your job and travel the world with a caravan and big top, how about trying to learn a circus art?

Quick Tip

- You don't even need any special 'equipment' to practice juggling. There's probably something suitable tucked away in a cupboard that you can learn with - balls, beanbags, scarves. If you get bored of that, how about learning to downward juggle with bouncy balls? Here are some other suggestions: -

    o   Tire your arms out poi spinning.
    o   Learn to unicycle.
    o   Try some devil/flower sticks.
    o   Already got the Diablo rhythm? Why not learn some tricks or try a smaller one (much harder to catch).
    o   Master the art of plate spinning (start with plastic ones please).

- You might reach a roadblock when you are teaching yourself some of these as a few can be hard to do unless you are shown how. See if you can find any books to help, or perhaps search for videos online. Use the same resources once you have found your confidence as they can help you to move to the next level and learn tricks.

- If you find yourself really enjoying any or all of the above, you could perhaps look into getting some training via a specialist school. I know of at least one in London, but you may find others nearer to you. They will be able to offer tips and advice to help you master some of the more difficult skills and it will also give you an opportunity to try others. Let's face it; how many of us can try a trapeze in our front room?

Inspired by the beauty and wonder of Cirque Du Soleil, I became hooked on the simple circus arts that usually only children decide to try. Who can think about depression when you have a plate spinning in each hand and another held between your knees!

I would spend hours alone in the park with my headphones in teaching myself how to poi spin, and it was one of the most soothing things I could have done to fight depression. The sound of the ribbons cutting through the air, to the feel of the muscles burning in my arms as I maintained the graceful movements. Even the transfixed smiles of passing children who gape at the bright colours in awe: each and every one gave me the distraction I needed.

Because I chose to learn at home instead of attending special classes (and they do exist) our living room became a circus-filled playground; enabling me to easily concentrate my energy towards something fun and rewarding instead of allowing it to channel itself along paths that I no longer frequent. Despite the lack of enthusiasm from my two cats, downward juggling became my circus trick of choice, although you might find yourself hooked on something completely different. Spinning plates to cheer yourself up might sound silly and childish, but I soon learnt that it is definitely worth giving it a go.

94 : KNOCK THEM DOWN

Ten-pin bowling can be a very satisfying distraction as well as being one that encourages you to be social. Depending on how many games you play and when, it can also be so knackering that you are too tired to even think about anything else except resting those bowling arms and getting into bed.

I personally believe that bowling is such a great addition to this book because it is very easy to get the hang of and is something that most people do enjoy. It is also an excellent stress reliever because you can lug that bowling ball down the lane as aggressively as you want and no one will look twice.

The only reason I ever used to dislike going bowling with my work colleagues was because I was rubbish at it; which made me uncomfortable because most of them were near pros. I never actually admitted this was the reason however, and instead used to head down to the local bowling alley with my best mate - who was just as bad at the game as me. Together, we would chuck heavy coloured balls into the gutter and laugh at how few strikes we would get between us.

Most of my bowling hours were late at night; when depression was most likely to bite me, and I would usually return home close to midnight feeling absolutely exhausted. I slept well and woke up looking forward to our next bowling night.

As a student who bowled during off-peak hours, my game was cheap enough to make bowling become a distraction that I could turn to quite often. It also helped that the local alley was open quite late.

Quick Tip

- Find out where your nearest bowling alley is and see if any of your friends would be interested in giving bowling a shot. Most people will be keen to meet up with friends for something social like this, and it can be nice knowing that you don't have to make too much conversation.

- Check to see if the bowling alley has any special events or offers on during the week. Many of them will have discounted nights or evenings where they turn the main lights off and light the lanes with fluorescents. I used to prefer those nights because I couldn't help but feel conscious of people watching us. In the dark, it doesn't matter quite as much. If you are self-conscious like me, perhaps you will find it more comfortable playing on the end lanes. Ask to be put in those ones when you pay for your game, or at least have a quick peek at the lanes to see which area looks quieter.

- If you can't find anyone interested in going bowling with you, there are computer games that simulate the experience (- technology never ceases to amaze!) Although these virtual games will never be quite the same as the real thing, the Wii version at least gets you up out of your seat and using your arm, whilst online games let you compete with your friends via the Internet.

95 : SEEK SOME THRILLS

I am a firm believer that once in a while we should all do something that we are afraid of. Learning to conquer our fears helps us to become stronger and more confident, no matter how trivial those fears may seem.

The adrenaline we naturally produce when we are scared is extremely powerful and greatly affects our mood. Often our lifestyle means that we are rarely in situations that get our hearts pumping in this way, and so it is down to us to put ourselves in them.

Your initial thought to the ideas listed might be a quick 'no way!' but trust me when I say they can all be wonderful distractions. Not only might you find that you enjoy thrill seeking, afterwards you might also feel a great sense of achievement from having given it a go. These are the kinds of emotions that depression struggles to strangle, and so they are perfect for arming yourself with.

Quick Tip

- Why not seek the thrills by doing one or all of the following: -

    o   Get on a roller coaster - It might be less scary than it looks.

- o   Book a bungee jump.
- o   Take part in an abseil.
- o   Find a place to micro-light.
- o   Enjoy the serenity of a glider flight - the absence of engine noise is extremely peaceful.
- o   Take a leap of faith with a skydive - you could even arrange to get sponsored and raise money for a worthy cause at the same time.
- o   Get up close and personal with a wild animal, such as a caged tiger or tank full of sharks.

I've done all except the bungee jump and I'm still here to tell the tales. I wouldn't even call myself an adrenaline-junkie; I just like to try new things.

Even if you find afterwards that you didn't enjoy them, these kinds of adventures make great conversation topics. After all, not all experiences in life have to be fun in order for them to be beneficial. I learnt more about myself from hating the single shark-dive than I ever did from years and years of loving theme park roller coasters.

Another important side effect you might find by putting yourself safely in situations where you are scared, is that death might not seem so attractive after all (notice I said safely!) I did many hair-raising things during the years when I was at my most suicidal, yet by doing them I discovered that deep down I didn't actually want to die. This is a natural instinct of course, but often we do need a subtle reminder.

96 : TURN THOSE FINGERS GREEN

I called in sick to work once partially because I genuinely didn't feel right, and partially because I was too depressed to do the things I knew would make me feel better. I was stuck in a vicious circle. I lay in bed feeling sick and hungry, I felt sick and hungry because I was too fed up with life to go downstairs and eat.

My flatmate eventually came in with a glass of water for me and to find out how I was doing. He had seen the face of depression many times before and he knew instantly that the physical sickness was only half the story. I eventually admitted to him that the urges to self-harm were getting stronger, and he responded by getting me outside.

I had bought a hundred daffodil bulbs on impulse in the supermarket a week before and they had sat in the shed ever since. Feeling guilty that they were being wasted, I armed myself with a small garden fork and attacked the mud patch that had once been a garden. Before long I was pulling out weeds, transplanting pot plants, and eagerly watching for daffodils to appear.

Quick Tip

- It may sound cliché, but taking the time and effort to nurture either your garden or some houseplants really changes how you feel about yourself. When you feel angry and frustrated, run around and dig up weeds, or pull slugs off your vegetable patch. You'll be amazed how satisfying it is. If you feel pointless and unloved, take pride in your pot plants and notice how much they grow.

When you care for something like a plant, they respond by looking healthy. Depression feels timeless: like nothing has changed nor ever will. As simple as this may sound, the subtle growth of a new leaf can help put time back in perspective.

I've had my mood gently lifted on many occasions just from seeing a new growth; like a gentle flower atop an unlikely cactus. Surrounding yourself with plants really can create a positive atmosphere, which in turn contributes to your state of mind. Not only that, but the oxygen is good for you!

I always thought that plants had no chance surviving around me due to my uncoordinated watering and lack of plant knowledge. That was until I found the cacti and the Internet. The cactus is a perfect starter plant because they really are hard to kill. With a bit of research online I could find out about caring for different varieties, and soon I was longing for more. Cacti also matched my self-harming nature perfectly because lets face it, I wasn't about to be put off by a few spines jabbing me in the hand.

I love how a cactus can look so butch and aggressive, yet so fragile and elegant. It goes without saying that I've even managed to kill a few cacti along the way, but the beauty of a plant is that you can always go and buy another one that will probably look near identical. Or perhaps next time you try and find one that is a little hardier, or better suited to your home.

There are so many possibilities that it is almost impossible not to be distracted by the humble plant.

FREE TO

97 : USE YOUR MEMBERSHIP

Ahh. Gym memberships. They are something most of us try out at some points in our lives, never use as much as we hoped, and are happy to cancel for the extra bit of cash each month.

I joined the gym to make use of the swimming pool, sauna and Jacuzzi, but felt awkward whilst doing the mandatory tour of the facilities. The introduction hour felt like a modern form of torture. I followed the staff member around and performed on cue; trying to keep my cool so that the more hardy gym-goers didn't point and laugh. There are machines in the gym that I still can't work out how to use or why, and the truth is, I'm happy not knowing.

As much as I would have to drag myself to the gym kicking and screaming like a rotten-toothed child on the way to the dentist, I had to admit there were benefits. Going swimming regularly is such a perfect distraction for me that it had to have its own chapter, but the gym had other uses too. I started taking dance classes which I enjoyed so much that I would be buzzing for hours; sometimes days after. I met likeminded people who were just as nervous about joining as I had been, and I found myself feeling more confident about my life in general. The cafe also served pretty nice toast.

Quick Tip

- If you are already a member of a gym, then go!

- If you've never quite had the courage to join, why not ask a friend to take the introductory tour with you? Even if you decide not to join, it can be good to see what kinds of facilities are available. You might even be able to pick up a day pass. Having another person there can also help you avoid feeling pressured by the sales pitch.

- How about trying something new at the gym? If you usually only think about torturing your body on the treadmill, have a look at what other machines you might be comfortable with. Perhaps there are classes that might take your fancy, or a pool where you can swim through the fog of depression.

Sometimes just trying something new; although a bit daunting at first, can be just the push we need into a more positive outlook - not to mention the physical health benefits I keep harping on about.

FREE

98 : BE IN THE AUDIENCE

It is one thing to watch a show on television, but it is something else to actually go and see it being filmed live in front of you. Some people become audience members because they want to see one of their favourite celebrities, but it is also worth doing this distraction just to see a television show from a different angle.

We went to watch 'The IT Crowd' being filmed in a studio just a few minutes from our home. Although I had never heard of the cast beforehand, after watching an entire series being filmed we felt a sort of connection to the show. Of course we were privy to comical moments that never made it past the edit suite and this made us feel as though we had been 'let in' on some of the jokes. When it finally aired a while after, I felt privileged to have already seen each episode and actually enjoyed watching it again; despite the fact I never usually watch T.V. much.

It might sound silly and obvious, but this kind of distraction helps you to concentrate on doing things each week and also gives you something to focus on for a few hours. It's a bonus if the show is a comedy, as we all know that laughter can be one of the most effective tools against negative influences.

Quick Tip

- If there are studios nearby, see if they are filming any shows that need audience members. Don't be put off if it's a new show or you've never heard of the people in it; this can be a great way to

239

discover new interests. Most tickets are allocated free on a first come basis, so apply quickly and get to the studio early. There are dedicated websites where you can apply for tickets and a quick search on Google should point you in the right direction.

If you do manage to watch something being filmed and you find out it's not your kind of show, don't be put off going to see something else another time. This distraction can be a bit hit and miss, but if it gets you out of the house for a couple of hours with a few mates, then this is also time well spent.

99 : SCORE A BIRDIE

To be completely honest with you, golf is probably one of the distractions at the bottom of my personal list, but I'm writing about it because I do still appreciate the value it holds for others.

I am a fan of anything that forces us to go outside because I truly believe that most of us are not getting enough fresh air and sunlight. If you live in the UK like I do, then sunlight for sure is something we need more of!

Working your way around the golf course can be extremely relaxing as they are often quiet, naturally calm places to be. Swinging that club is also a great way to release that pent-up anger or frustration, and the golf ball isn't going to judge you if you take your feelings out on it. So you might have to do a bit of searching before you can continue your game; but this is all part of the fun, right?

Quick Tip

- If you are already a member of a golf club, get down there and distract yourself. Call up your regular golfing buddies and see if anyone fancies a round or two.

- If regular golf really isn't your cup of tea, don't cast mini-golf aside with it (or crazy golf as some prefer to call it). Although in a somewhat different league, mini-golf also makes a great distraction and has just the same benefits; only cheaper and less exclusive. My friends and I always have great fun trying to hit those golf balls into the tunnels that are invariably clogged with leaves, and end up laughing about how difficult some of those courses can be. It doesn't matter if you get a hole in seventeen, as long as you are distracted doing it.

- Putting ranges can be good fun even if you wouldn't consider yourself a golfer, and are an excellent way to relieve stress. Tire yourself out by hitting those balls as hard as you can.

- As a last ditch effort to interest you in this distraction, remember that there are loads of great computer games based around golf. If you own a console such as the Wii, then you will even have to get off the sofa to play them.

100 : SWIM YOUR WORRIES AWAY

After years battling with depression, most of the negative emotions that I am left with now are concerns over the way I look - or at least how I feel that I look. To cut it short, I lack confidence because I'm not as slim as I used to be, and as I age, I naturally notice my unfit body more and more.

However mature we are, exercise is an excellent way to introduce positive feeling and it will most likely have a knock-on effect on the type of lifestyle you lead. I always notice how much more healthy the foods are that I choose after I've been exercising. Eating well, in turn, encourages me to exercise in the first place.

My friend and I had a regular slot every other Friday night when we would drive to a large leisure centre and spend hours swimming, relaxing in the Jacuzzi and sauna, or teasing each other to jump into the freezing plunge pool. The weekend following this evening I would always feel positive and full of energy and wouldn't grimace at the body looking back at me from the mirror. It's only now that we've not been able to keep to our swimming night schedule over the last few months that I've noticed my negative way of seeing things has crept back to me.

Going swimming is an excellent distraction because it can be a social event just for adults, an excuse to take the kids out, or simply a chance for you to exercise quietly by yourself. There were many nights when I would head to the leisure centre alone; armed with a waterproof case and headphones for my iPod, so that I could immerse myself in Cirque du Soleil music whilst I paddled around the noisy main pool. No one would bother me and it didn't matter how rubbish I felt at the beginning of the day, I would come home from the pool feeling warm, snug, relaxed and ready for sleep.

Although my trips to the pool were not frequent enough for me to suddenly notice myself losing weight and becoming strong and fit, the effect it would have was on the way I 'saw' myself. That is, my mind felt healthier, and this is the very reason why this distraction is highly recommended. As well as being good for your physical health, swimming is soothing, relaxing and peaceful; even more so if your pool includes other spa facilities.

Quick Tip

- A simple swim session can be quite cheap at your local pool, so do check to see if they are open at a time to suit you. Some larger pools open for longer and often have other facilities available such as a gym or spa. Perhaps you can combine this distraction with other forms of exercise? Just make sure there are no classes scheduled otherwise you might find most, or all of the pool is closed to the public.

- Try not to let your mind convince you that you are too embarrassed to go swimming. I always feel self-conscious in my swimwear, but I soon forget about it once I'm in the water. Going swimming regularly can be a nice excuse to invest in a new bikini and that often helps me feel a bit more confident also. Perhaps you will feel the same?

- If you don't feel quite up to going to a pool alone, see if a friend will come with you. Just as I did - maybe after a few sessions you will find that you happy to swim by yourself on those occasions when your friend can't make it. Try and make a plan to go frequently, even if you don't perhaps think you feel like it. Often I'd be tempted not to bother, but having someone else to spur you on will mean that you can help each other find enthusiasm. Once you are there; as is often the case, you'll probably enjoy it more than you think. It's all about slowly gaining confidence and getting yourself into a bit of an exercise routine.

- If you've never learnt to swim or if water still frightens you, perhaps it is time to join a class. Whether you are taking to water for the first time or feel as though you need a few brush-up lessons, having a regular class can also be a great distraction - as mentioned in idea number 91.

- Even if you know where your local swimming pool is, don't forget to have a look to see what others are about. You might find one that has a wider choice of classes or sauna's etc, or perhaps offers something fun and different such as a wave-machine, slides, open-air or heated pool.

Sophia Gill

101 : SEE THE WORLD

Travelling has pretty much become the thing that I live for and after years of depressive spending, holidays are where my salary is spent now.

Although I am perhaps more greedy than most when it comes to seeing new places, I cannot emphasise enough how valuable this has been in terms of my recovery. Each of my trips; whether they have been a simple weekend away or weeks travelling to distant lands, have given me focus in my life; something to look forward to if you will.

Once an extremely shy, completely dependent and fearful person, the new experiences and insight I gained from travelling gave me the self-confidence and bravery to eventually holiday in Egypt alone. This was a place that I was fascinated with and scared of for years, but I never once imagined that my first ever visit would be without someone else to psychologically prop me up.

Whilst it obviously wasn't holidays alone that helped me to quit my self-harm, pack up my troubles and declare myself depression-free, what travelling did do at a basic level was open my eyes to all of the better things, more amazing places, tastier food and nicer people that were in the world.

Despite a touch of 'the grass is always greener', it was the hope - which certain things, people and places sparked inside of me, that became a major factor in my recovery. I found myself planning to return to favourite places; hoping to share my adventures with loved ones, and longing for more chances to experience other parts of the world. These hopes were firm ideas for my future, standing tall amongst a haze of depressive thoughts. When all else was destroyed by depression, my travel plans stood strong and proud, as clear reminders of more positive times.

Travelling also taught me many things about myself, which I never even considered or dared to believe. I wasn't as scared of being alone as I thought I would be. I was more able to cope with the culture shock than I ever imagined, and I enjoyed a far wider variety of food than I would normally have tried from staying at home. These were all valuable life lessons important to me - and who I've become, and yet it is only with Hindsight that I learnt the true depth of the decisions I made to travel. The independence especially was a surprise bi-product of my wish to simply get away from it all.

My holidays now are rarely about spending time that isn't just at work. They are about finding my strengths and weaknesses, testing my tolerance level and patience, and forcing myself to step outside of my comfort zone. No wonder I always come back feeling exhausted!

Quick Tip

- If you are like many of the people I work with and never use your full holiday allowance because you don't see the point, I urge you to properly plan a decent holiday. If you struggle to find inspiration, pop into a travel agency and ask them for ideas. Browse through their brochures or website and see what takes your fancy.

- If booking a holiday has never been much of a problem for you, but you tend to stick to places you know - now is the time to try something new. Is there anywhere you'd love to go but have perhaps have put the idea aside due to financial complications or fear? Why not plan a trip well in advance so that you have enough time to save for it. Travel agents won't send you anywhere that is dangerous, so take a leap of faith and follow their recommendations. Places a little bit further from home might be a culture shock, but there can be so much to learn from the experience. The sights, food, people and countryside can be unlike anything you have ever seen.

- Travelling doesn't have to cost your entire pay packet so keep an eye out for special offers. Flights will vary on a daily basis and hotels do offer free nights or other discounts. Long gone are the days when you have to book last-minute to get the best prices. Sometimes the exact opposite is true.

- Remember that a holiday doesn't have to mean lazing around by the pool all day every day, nor does it mean rushing around ticking off every sight possible. If you usually do one, how about trying the other? Or maybe even mix it up a little and visit somewhere you can do a bit of both.

- If you already have a trip booked, remind yourself how much you are looking forward to it. If I'm having a bad day, sometimes I will look at new reviews online about the hotel I'll be heading to; helping re-ignite that excitement I felt when I first booked it. Needless to say, I do tend to always have one trip to look forward to at any one point in time, but on the rare occasion that I don't, I'm either in the middle of planning, or looking at photos of the last one.

Sophia Gill

EPILOGUE

I truly believe that one of the most important things to hold on to when you are making any sort of recovery; is the understanding that it will take time - often a lot of it. I endured thousands of cuts all over my body over a solid span of eleven years before I realised I was getting anywhere. Even then, I still self-harmed occasionally until the day I could honestly say that I was over the addiction.

There is no single piece of advice that I could write, or a solitary distraction that will be your miracle cure. You have to think of this as layers. Every single idea in this book is there for the purpose of helping you find strength and value in yourself. From encouraging you to step out of your comfort zone, to introducing you to a new passion; each distraction has the possibility to re-enforce your defences so that soul-destroyers struggle to find a way in.

If you keep using these distractions and continue to explore new territory, eventually you will notice that the positives are taking up more time than the negatives. The point is that you probably won't even see this strength growing; but you must have faith that it is. One day you will look back and think 'oh - how did that happen?'

I am so ridiculously different from the dysfunctional, melancholic girl that I used to be, that I often find it impossible to accept that I am in fact the same person. When I started doing interviews on television to try and explain self-harm to the masses, it didn't even occur to me that this was something I would have run a mile from years previously. I distinctly remember one occasion when traffic caused me to turn up slightly late for a live BBC1 news programme and I was put on air without even knowing the kinds of questions that would be asked of me. Surprisingly, I didn't panic, clam up or freak out, and instead managed to remain coherent and true to expectations.

There is not a single reason in the world why you couldn't be the strong, happy person that you hope and deserve to be. Speaking as someone who has gone from being too shy and depressed to tell my psychiatrist that I had a bad day, to being able to talk about it freely with anyone at any time; I genuinely want to reassure you that this strength is possible.

All I have ever wanted from my experience of spending so many years just one step away from suicide; from all the blood shed and tears lost; from the hurt, anger and agonising hours wishing it were all over - is to simply help someone else.

I have analysed over and over the process that led me to this point and I am positive that well-timed distractions are the all-important first step. Naturally you must have the desire to change and get better, but without that I doubt you would have even given my words a second look.

You may have reached the end of this book, but I truly hope that it has opened doors to a new beginning and inspired you to keep fighting. I know soul-destroyers feel endless and I understand just how arduous and debilitating they are, but this feeling really isn't forever.

FURTHER READING

For further information on the ideas behind this book, and details of
Sophia's latest work, please visit
www.DistractionsfromDepression.com

To contact the author, please email
info@DistractionsfromDepression.com

For more information on SANE, please visit **www.sane.org.uk**

SANE

60762976R00150

Made in the USA
Middletown, DE
04 January 2018